Offspring of God

Origin & Manifestation of the New Creation

Rudi Louw

The Holy Scriptures are just that, HOLY.

Statements enclosed in brackets were inserted
into Scripture quotations to add emphasis or to
clarify the meaning of what is being said in
those scriptures.

The integrity of God's Word to man was not
compromised in any way. Due care and
diligence was cautiously exercised to keep the
Word of Truth intact.

Table of Content

The Marvel of the Holy Bible

1. Uninterrupted Theme and Inspired Thought

It took *1,500 years* to compile the Holy Bible, involving *more than 40 different authors*. Yet the theme and inspired thought of Scripture continues *uninterrupted* from author to author, from beginning till end.

2. Absence of Mythical Stories

Compare philosophies and theories about creation in the Middle East, Europe, Asia, Africa, and Latin America and you'll find mythical scenarios: gods feuding and cutting up other gods to form the heavens and the earth, etc.

In ancient Greek mythology, the Greeks see Atlas carrying the earth on his shoulders. In India, Hindus believe eight elephants carry the earth on their backs.

But in contrast, Job, the oldest book in the Holy Bible, declares that, *"God suspends the earth on nothing."*(Job 26:7)

This was said millennia before Isaac Newton discovered the invisible laws of gravity that delicately balance every planet and sun in its individual circuit.

Contrary to every other ancient attempt to give a creation account, *the Holy Bible pictures the creation of the earth in a very scientific manner.*

For example, in Genesis Chapter One, the continents are lifted from the seas, then vegetation is formed and later animal life, all reproducing *'according to its own kind'*, **thus recognizing the fixed genetic laws.** In addition, we have the bringing forth of man and woman, *all done by God in a dignified and proper manner, without mythological adornments.*

The balance or remainder of the Holy Bible follows suite.

The narratives are **true historical documents***, faithfully reflecting society and culture* **as history and archaeology would discover them thousands of years later. Not only is the Holy Bible historically accurate, it is also reliable when it deals with scientifically proven subjects.**

It was never intended to be a textbook on history, science, mathematics, or medicine. *However, when its writers touch on these subjects,* **they often state facts that scientific advancement would not reveal, or**

6

even consider, until thousands of years later.

While many have doubted the accuracy of the Holy Bible, time and continued research have consistently demonstrated that the Word of God is better informed than its critics.

3. Intactness

Of all the ancient works of substantial size, *the Holy Bible survives intact, against all odds and expectations.*

Compared with other ancient writings, the Holy Bible has more manuscripts as evidence to support it than any ten pieces of classical literature combined!

The plays of William Shakespeare, for instance, were written about four hundred years ago, after the invention of the printing press. Many of his original writings and words have been lost in numerous sections, *yet the Holy Bible's uncanny preservation has weathered thousands of years of wars, contradictions, persecutions, fires and invasions.*

Through the centuries Jewish scribes have preserved the Holy Bible's Old Covenant text, **such as no other manuscripts have ever been preserved. They kept tabs on every letter, syllable, word and paragraph.** *They*

7

continued from generation to generation to appoint and train special groups of men within their culture **whose sole duty it was to preserve and transmit these documents <u>with perfect accuracy and fidelity</u>.**

Who ever bothered to count the letters, syllables, or words of Plato, Aristotle, or Seneca for that matter?

When it comes to the New Testament, the actual number of preserved manuscripts is so great that it becomes overwhelming. *There are more than 5,680 Greek manuscripts, more than 10,000 Latin Vulgate manuscripts and at least 9,300 other versions. Further still, there exists an additional 25,000 manuscript copies of portions of the New Testament.* **No other document of antiquity even begins to approach such numbers.**

The closest in comparison is Homer's <u>Iliad</u>, with only 643 manuscripts. The first complete work of Homer only dates back to the 13th century.

4. Unmatched Accuracy in Predictive Foretelling

The Holy Bible is unmatched in accuracy in predictive foretelling. No other ancient work succeeds in this, or even begins to attempt this.

Other books such as the Koran, the Book of Mormon, and parts of the Veda claim divine inspiration; *but none of these books contain predictive foretelling.*

This one undeniable fact we know for certain: *While microscopic scrutiny would show up the imperfections, blemishes, and defects of any work of man, <u>it magnifies the beauties and perfection of God</u>. Just as every flower displays in accurate detail the reflection and perfection of beauty, <u>so does the Word of Truth when it is scrutinized</u>.*

Historian Philip Schaff wrote:

"Without money and weapons, Jesus the Christ conquered more millions than Alexander, Caesar, Muhammad, and Napoleon. Without science and learning, He (Jesus the Christ) *shed more light on things human and divine than all philosophers and scholars combined. Without the eloquence of schools, He* (Jesus the Christ) *spoke such words of life as was never spoken before or since and produced effects which lie beyond the reach of orator or poet. Without writing a single line, He* (Jesus the Christ) *set more pens in motion and furnished themes for more sermons, orations, discussions, learned volumes, works of art, and songs of praise* **than the whole army of great men of ancient and modern times combined.***" (The Person of Christ, p33. 1913)*

Today, there are literally billions of Bibles in more than 2,000 languages.

Isn't it about time you find out what it really has to say?

Hey listen, the Holy Bible is all about Jesus, the Messiah, the Christ...

...and everything about Jesus Christ is really about YOU!!

Study Tips:

Read 2 Corinthians 5:14, 16, 18, 19, and 21.

In the light of these Scriptures, it should be obvious that, if you want to study the Holy Bible, *you should study it in the light of Mankind's redemption!*

Feed daily on **redemption realities** found in the book of Acts, in Romans Chapters One through Eight, and in Ephesians, Colossians, and Galatians. These realities may also be found in 1 Peter Chapter One, 2 Peter Chapter One, James Chapter 1, as well as in 1 and 2 Corinthians.

Foreword

Thank you for taking the time to read this book.

Let me start off by saying that *I am totally addicted to my Daddy's love for me.*

I am in love with Jesus Christ, *and that is enough for me!*

The love of God is so much more than a doctrine, a philosophy, or a theory. It is so much more and goes so much deeper than knowledge; it way surpasses knowledge. *We are talking heart language here.*

Therefore this book was not written to impress intellectuals with knowledge and philosophy, theologians with theories and doctrine, nor English majors with grammar and spelling for that matter. *So if you come up with any other definitions or find any language inaccuracies, please don't use it to disqualify Love's own message I bring to you in this book.*

I write *to impact people's hearts,* to make them see the mysteries that have been hidden in Father God's heart concerning Christ Jesus, and actually *concerning THEM,* so as to arrest their conscience with it, *that I may introduce them to their original design and to their true selves,* **and present them to themselves**

perfect in Christ Jesus *and set them apart unto Him* **in love,** as a chaste virgin.

We are involved with the biggest romance of the ages. Therefore this book cannot be read as you would a novel: *casually.* It is not a cleverly devised little myth or fable. **It contains revelation and** *truth* **into some things you may or may not have considered before.**

It is not blasphemy or error though. *It is the TRUTH of God, ultimate TRUTH, and therefore has direct bearing upon YOUR life.* **The Word and the Spirit are my witness** *to the reality of these things!*

Be like the people of Berea the apostle Paul ministered to in Acts 17:11. Open yourself up to study the revelation contained in this book *to discover for yourself the reality of these things*.

Be forewarned! Do not become guilty of the sins of the Pharisees, **or you too will miss out on the depth of fulfillment God Himself, who is LOVE, wants to give you**.

Jesus said of the Pharisees and Sadducees that they strain out every little gnat, BUT swallow whole camels. What He meant by that is that *some people seem to have it all together when it comes to doctrine and they love to argue.* **It makes them feel important, but it is nothing other than EMPTY religious and intellectual pride.** *They know the*
12

Scriptures in and out, and YET they are still so IGNORANT about **REAL TRUTH** *that is only* **found in LOVE.** *They are still so ignorant and indifferent* **towards the things that REALLY MATTER.** *They are always arguing over the use of* every little jot and tittle *and over the meaning and interpretation of* every word of Scripture.

The exact thing they accuse everyone else of doing though, the precise thing they judge everyone else for, *they are actually doing themselves.* That is **they often downright misinterpret and twist what is being said, making a big deal of insignificant things while obscuring or weakening God's real truth: the truth of His LOVE.** *They are always majoring on minors* **because they do not understand the heart of God** **and therefore they constantly miss the whole point of the message.**

Paul himself said it so beautifully,

"...the letter kills but **the Spirit BRINGS LIFE;"**

"...knowledge puffs up, but **LOVE EDIFIES."**

I say again:

Allow yourself to get caught up in the revelation I am about to share. Open yourself up to study the insight contained in this book, *not only with a desire to gain knowledge, but also with anticipation* **to hear from Father God yourself;**

…to encounter Him through His Word;

…and to embrace truth, in order to know and believe the LOVE God has for <u>you</u>, so that you may get so caught up in it, *that you too may receive from Him LOVES' impartation of LIFE.*

This revelation contains within it the voice and call of LOVE Himself to every human being on the face of this earth. *If you take heed to it, it is custom designed and guaranteed to forever alter and enrich your life!*

Acknowledgment

I want to acknowledge and thank one of my mentors in the faith, Francois du Toit, for blessing and impacting me with revelation knowledge.

I borrowed the portion on *"The Marvel of the Holy Bible"* from his website: http://www.MirrorWord.net, as students so often feel they have a right to do with things that come from teachers they respect. Just as Galatians 6:6 says, *"Let him who is taught the Word share in all good things with him who teaches."*

To all our dear friends and family, for all the love and support, and to Chase Aderhold and all those who helped me with this project:

THANK YOU!

And, especially to my wife, Carmen;

For keeping me real and being my companion in life and partner in ministry:

I love and appreciate you so very much!

Introduction

As an introduction to our subject in this book, the following thoughts were mostly taken from my friend Andre Rabe's book, Imagine, then modified and rearranged before being added to my thoughts.

In speaking about the eternal, timeless realm in which God dwells, we should not really use our time related terms and tenses. **Eternity has its own language, and it is different from the language of time!**

When we speak of the eternal timeless realm, we speak about a realm decidedly different from what we normally experience in this physical world. In time things decay. In eternity there is no decay. In time there is past, present, and future. In timeless eternity there is no past or future as we observe it in our world, only something similar to what we call the present.

Time began. Eternity is.

Time is often defined as a sequence of events. There certainly are also events in eternity, as seen from 2 Timothy 1:9, but these events are not bound to the past or the future. If there is a sequence, it is based on the significance of the event rather than *'time.'*

17

While thinking with a mind bound to time, **it is difficult to grasp eternal truth, or eternal reality. It is a different language!** It takes revelation to see things from God's eternal perspective instead of seeing from a time-bondage perspective. **Only the Holy Spirit can open our eyes to the Father's eternal perspective.**

In short, in order for us to comprehend timeless eternity and to understand its language, it will take an impartation of insight and revelation into the knowledge of God by the Holy Spirit Himself. It is the revelation which comes from Him alone that saves us and lifts us out of our time-bound thinking and a time-bound mentality.

We exist within the context of time. Even our language is mostly bound to time. But God wants us to understand and communicate freely in His language, in the language of that eternal spirit realm, of that eternal spirit truth, that eternal spirit reality.

Life is like a massive movie that we joined halfway through the screening. Just imagine walking into a cinema, half-way through the film. It will probably take you a while to figure out the plot and to understand the characters, having missed the beginning.

You see, we have all entered a story that began long before we were born. We are part of a very, very big story, written by God

Himself. **This story began before creation.** Although we, you and I, entered this story rather late, the Director wants to let us in on the whole story **so we can understand our importance and become a significant part of the story**.

The secret of understanding this story and being able to speak its language and communicate its plot from beginning to end is not out of reach to any one of us. God has placed that language; He has placed eternity into our hearts, so that we too can have access into those realms of timeless eternity, beyond the here and now of our existence. (Read Ecclesiastes 3:11, 2 Timothy 1:9, and Ephesians 1:4 & 5)

So, in God, there exists a timeless realm not subject to decay, a spirit realm of spiritual reality; a realm of Spirit Truth. What happens in that timeless realm is immutable. What is declared in that realm is unchangeable and what is given to us in that realm is irreversible, *"for God's gifts and His call are irrevocable."* (Romans 11:29. Read also Isaiah 46:10)

When John writes about the Word that was in the beginning (John 1:1), he refers to this eternal, timeless realm of God. He refers to an eternal event, to a conversation and decision within the Godhead; a forever unchangeable decree that was made in God, concerning us, in that eternal, timeless realm. He refers to an eternal reality, to something much greater than a time-related event.

The word he uses is *'ar-khay'* which means chief (in various applications of order, time, place, or rank), beginning, first (estate), magistrate, power, principality, principle, and rule. **So he speaks of that which is most important, most significant, and most central.**

John is referring to the beginning of all beginnings, the origin of all origins, the first cause, and the very essence of God's motivation. We are talking about an eternal, timeless event, an event that is forever valid, forever present! God's eternal motivation, His choice and decree, is new every morning. It is as vibrant, real, urgent, and every bit as true and inspiring, and truth right now, as it has always been. The incarnation, life, death, and resurrection of Jesus Christ happened within our time, but it was and is a manifestation of an eternal event, an eternal reality and truth within God.

His appearance revealed what has always been true. The exact mystery hidden in the heart of God for ages and generations was and is finally made known in our dimension of time and space. The message of Christ is nothing less than the unveiling of God's reality, the truth as He sees it.

We can no longer think of God apart from His revelation of Himself in this event. Neither can we think of ourselves apart from God's revelation of us in this event. **God bound Himself inseparably to us. And when the Creator became part of creation, He confirmed it.** Our very existence in this time-bound dimension was forever challenged and altered by this act, by this event that took place in the fullness of time or also known as the end of time. You see, time itself as a whole has been redeemed, *as God and Man are revealed face to face in the man Jesus Christ,* who is then also resurrected from the dead and eternally raised up, seated as the right hand of God, seated in the eternal spirit realm of spiritual reality and eternal truth.

He is eternally present, the new and yet old, but also the newly revealed **reality of our existence! He is the ultimate representation of the reality of God, and the ultimate representation of the reality of Man.** What He accomplished, what He revealed and then reaffirmed in the work of redemption, can mean nothing less than the total reconciliation of God and Man. You were in Christ, you were therefore also in His death, in His resurrection, and in His ascension **because of that timeless eternal association and connection from before time began. In Christ you are confronted with the reality of your eternal identity in God and with the reality of your salvation in every way from a time-bound mentality and existence. We**

can do nothing against this truth, only for this truth!

To have faith is to consistently live in the awareness of what God is aware of. Faith is not something we generate ourselves. The truth and faith of God is contained within the declaration of this eternal gospel. **We can receive it or reject it, but we can never invalidate it or replace it with our own persuasions and perspective. It is a timeless and eternal language with an eternal perspective.**

If it seems that some Scriptures contradict this eternal perspective from which I often write, and from which I wrote this book, it is only because, quite often, the only way God can communicate with natural-minded and fall-minded and law-minded people is through that language which they understand: a time-bound, law-bound, fall-of-Adam-bound language.

For instance, when God addresses the Hebrew mind, He uses the sacrificial system and law-bound language in order to communicate and relate to the Jews. Even in the New Testament, even in the book of Hebrews, He explains Christ to them from that time and law-bound perspective, in law-bound, time-bound language they can relate to, just in order to get them to understand eternal realities.

In many places in Scripture, He talks about cleansing His own mind by blotting out sin and remembering it no more. Yet in the eternal realm, God's mind remained cleansed in spite of the fall, because as far as that timeless, eternal realm is concerned, the Lamb (Christ) was slain from before time began. And God, who sees the end from the beginning and lives outside of time, had already made His mind up about Man and had chosen to love Man.

God's truth is eternal, and thus He has never been confused or needed to repent and change His mind or cleanse His mind from anything. God is not a man that He should be taken off guard and have to adjust His perspective just a little bit. He is not time-bound like us, whom often unexpectedly find out that we have believed a lie, or a half-truth, and that we have been deceived.

"God is light and in Him is no darkness at all."

"He is not a man that He should lie; nor is He a son of man that He should repent."

Our whole identity and our whole existence, our eternal identity and existence are defined in Christ and by Christ, before and after the work of redemption. In Him all things find their meaning. **The total summary and conclusion of Man's identity and worth is found in Him. He was and is now again after His ascension, forever seated and at rest in this reality!**

We are included in Him and seated with Him –
we no longer have to live within the
contradiction to eternal reality which entered
the world through Adam. For we have an
origin that began before Adam **and was
revealed and totally restored in Christ to the
fullness of its glory.**

Let me just add this one more thing before I get
condemned and stoned, just as Stephen was,
by law-minded people trapped in a time-bound
existence and definition of life.

We are often asked two hugely pertinent
questions:

What does it mean to be "in" Christ?

And does it even matter what we believe?

It is obvious they misunderstand what we teach
because of their traditional religious teachings
and understanding.

Here is our answer:

If by "in" Christ we mean that Christ is the One
who gives life and breath to everyone (*"He
Himself gives to all men, life, breath, and all
other things."* Acts 17:25),

Then YES, in that context, we believe He is
present everywhere.

If by "in" Christ we mean that nothing can exist without Him, then YES, we believe He sustains everything, the whole universe!

However, and listen carefully now…

If by "in" Christ we mean a living relationship, a living union between Christ and a person whereby Christ can express Himself through that person;

…**then NO, we don't believe Christ is in everyone, in this context.**

Darkness cannot fellowship with light!

What a person believes absolutely matters!

Faith releases the benefit of the truth. (Hebrews 4:2).

This *"Word of Truth"*, this *"Gospel of Your Salvation"*, **is first and foremost a declaration of the truth as God knows it. It is the declaration of His persuasion. In it you are confronted with the reality of your salvation in Christ Jesus.** When you and I are presented with the reality of what God has to say about our timeless, eternal identity in Him, and with what He has done for and with us in Christ to restore us fully to that timeless eternal identity, **it does not remove the need for faith. In fact, IT GREATLY INTENSIFIES IT!**

When we see the **GREATER reality** of God's opinion and truth about us and what He has done for us and to us, to restore us, and how it contrasts with the **LESSER reality** of our experience, **it creates a clear confrontation.**

Do we want to live in God's reality revealed, or continue in the chaos and deception of our own opinions? Once we've seen God's eternal, timeless truth about ourselves, we cannot reject it without rejecting our own existence. He chose us and demonstrated His choice of us in Christ beyond doubt. How can we do anything but make a decision for Him when we realize His decision for us?!

His decision was to give Himself to us completely and to lavish His love upon us all! In becoming a man, He made known that His will and purpose have forever been and will forever be **to be totally united with man!** It is on the basis of this decision of God, already made before the ages about us, and made known in time, in Christ, to us, **that we are enabled to make a decision for Him.**

Seeing people come into a living relationship with Christ through the declaration of this eternal good news *is the greatest privilege there is!*

"How grateful we are
to God,

the father of
our lord Jesus Christ,

who has brought **us**
into every blessing
of the spirit

in the heavenly places
(the invisible realm
of **eternal realities**)

through **our union with**

Christ Jesus."

"Even before
the fall of the world
God **chose us**

and **associated us** in Christ

and thus called us out
into a holy and blameless
standing before Him

without any evidence

against us

to limit His approval of us

(God preserved the master
copy of man
in Christ
in spite of the fall.

Thus the implications of the
fall is completely canceled out.)

His eternal love plan and
destiny (all along) **for us**

has been **our full adoption as sons** through Jesus Christ unto Himself.

This was according to the delight of His will

which will be celebrated

to the praise and appreciation **of His glorious intention in His grace**

by which He has taken _us_ into His favor

30

through our union with the Beloved."

"We are the end-product of His workmanship,

created in Christ Jesus

unto love and good works.

These good works **are merely the fruit** of the new creation

according to God's original design."

- Ephesians 1:3-6 and
- Ephesians 2:10

Chapter 1

We are God's Image & Likeness

I am so glad that the gospel confirms God's faithfulness. And so as we study the Scriptures together our hearts bear witness to God who reveals Himself in absolute integrity.

It's so good to see that in His gospel contained there in the Scriptures, God reveals His intention in such a way that He leaves no room for misunderstanding.

What a joy to discover that the Holy Spirit has all the competence and all the qualification to communicate the deep things of God, and communicate it in such a way that deep calls unto deep.

I am so thankful that God's word, God's gospel, does not appeal, in the first place, to an intellectual, academic understanding, but it appeals to the deep within the heart of Man.

How amazing it is to find Paul addressing a very heathen audience in the book of Acts, Chapter Seventeen, **and his focus in addressing them is in reference to them as the offspring of God!**

I am so glad that he *knew and understood* that even though they stood there in front of him with no prior education in the Christian faith, no prior, so-called, Christian religious preparation, *he knew and understood* that the years of ignorance, the years of hostile tradition contrary to and in resistance to the truth, *could not keep their hearts from responding to the voice of God's appeal.*

He said to them that,

"Even your own poets have tapped into an understanding that reveals that in Him we live, we move, we have our being."

And listen as I say again: he is not addressing a Christian audience there. He is not addressing an Evangelical and Charismatic audience there. He is addressing a very heathen audience that had never before that day even heard of the gospel of the grace of God. Paul made a very clear appeal to a specific likeness within them that associated them with more than what their imagination allowed them to see in their works of art and their representations in gold and in silver, to give expression, to give tangible definition to their thought and idea of God.

Paul revealed to them that they carried all along, within them, all the reference Man ever needs to know Him; the only one, true, and living God.

I am so glad that God has overlooked the times of ignorance. He has overlooked our time of ignorance, yours and mine as well.

Hallelujah!

I am so glad God has chosen to overlook that which hinders Man and limits Man, and He has chosen to rescue Man in his perceiving of His Creator again ...and by implication his perceiving of himself again also, as in a mirror.

Chapter 2

Not an Inferior Reflection of God

In our study in this book I want us to consider what Paul said there in Ephesians 3:10, when he made the statement that, *"**We were created in Christ Jesus.**"* I want us to take a look at these things and discover for ourselves the concept of **the New Creation** together.

Now, in studying the New Creation, we cannot but begin with *that which was from the beginning.* I say again, in order to thoroughly understand these things we have to go back to the time before time began, to eternity itself, *to the very origin of the New Creation: **the heart of God**.*

You see, **God knew Man intimately** before Man was. God wasn't in an experimental mode one day, when the sudden and rather novel thought came to Him of creating a being that would dwell within a physical realm, and seeing that being, called Man, **as an intimate associate and companion** to Himself. God had a very exact, very accurately defined understanding within His being, within the depth of His thought, that this being, called Man, this new creature, would not be an inferior reflection of what God saw within Himself.

Now my wife is a very good cook and loves to experiment in the kitchen. As for me however, I know very little about experimenting in the kitchen, and I really can't show my skills there. But I can tell you that we have witnessed our experiments in the kitchen together, in the early days of our marriage and even now from time to time, and it's amazing how often we have been disappointed, even with Carmen's skill at cooking, when it doesn't look quite like the recipe foretold. I mean we have all these wonderful Betty Crocker cooking books with these glossy pictures that are so perfect and mouth-watering to look at. I mean it's finger-licking-good to even just see the pictures... ha... ha... ha...

And there in those books you have listed and on display all the required ingredients. And so we take our first bold attempt to take all those ingredients and put them together, expecting the very same, you know, an equal display of the picture revealed in the recipe. But often the disappointment is more than what even your faith can handle ...and so the garbage can had to handle it... ha... ha... ha...

But in dealing with the thoughts of God, with an idea that has its origin in the *"Logos",* in a thought, in the very logic of God, in a conversation, in a Word **that was from the beginning,** *we are not dealing with a clumsy* *effort of God, seeking to somehow reproduce Himself and reproduce His thinking in a being that would be a lesser expression of what His thought knew.*

In dealing with the New Creation and discovering the origin of the New Creation together, **we need to discover that its *"newness"* is not measured in time or dispensation,** because it has its origin in the beginning. Its origin is in the Ancient Of Days.

You see, in dealing with this topic of the New Creation, we are involved with a timeless being. And in all eternity God could never be older than age 33... ha... ha... ha...

Let me tell you, God does not desire to express Himself in a being, within the dispensation of time, where time would be able to present any threat or where history would be able to present enough contradiction to either diminish or extinguish the replica of God's likeness, the replica of all that His thought saw and knew about this creature called Man.

It is truly wonderful as an individual to discover and to know that our origin, as well as our association with Him, has a history to it that is larger than all of time, than dispensationalism, than this modern age, than all of church history and church doctrine, larger even than all of Mankind's religious history combined. It is large enough for this being, called Man, *to be an eternal one **and to remain such in time.***

Because of our history, because of our origin, because of our eternal association with Him, neither time nor history would interfere with this eternal being, God's New Creation, which stands forever in a fellowship with the Godhead where all of God is reflected within this being.

Chapter 3

Associated IN HIM

I want to draw your attention to Ephesians Chapter One, and I'll start with Verse Three.

"Blessed be the God and father of our Lord Jesus Christ..."

"Our Lord Jesus Christ" **has His origin in God. God fathered Jesus Christ. The man, Jesus Christ, therefore has a God and a father.**

Hebrews 2:11 confirms this by saying,

*"**Both** He who sanctifies and those who are sanctified **share the same origin.**"*

That is why if you continue to read there in Hebrews 2 you will see that **Jesus is not ashamed to call Man His brother.**

*...**Because they come out of the same mold; out of the same womb,***

*...**they were formed in the same thought;***

*...**they have the same origin as their reference, the Logos, the eternal One.***

Paul continues to say there in Ephesians 1:3 that,

"He, this Father ...has blessed us in Christ Jesus with every spiritual blessing in the heavenly places (in the unseen realm of spirit realities).*"*

Now if He has blessed us in Christ Jesus with every spiritual blessing in the heavenly places, in that unseen spirit realm of reality, in our very spirit, *then we may safely conclude that **Man lacks in nothing!*** Being blessed with every spiritual blessing, *with all that God could communicate in terms of blessing,* **leaves Man complete!**

You see, we sing with Moses that song, ***"Ascribe greatness** to our God..."* Our praise finds its definition in the greatness of the God we are dealing with. And we see His greatness revealed in His workmanship. *"**His work is perfect**..."* - Deuteronomy 32:3 & 4

Paul continues there in Verse Four of Ephesians Chapter One,

*"Even as **He chose us** in Him..."*

The Mirror Translation uses the phrase, *"...**associated us in Christ**".* Can you see in this thought that is communicated here that God does not see an inferior creature to His Son? No. God sees a being, a Mankind associated in the same blessing that His Son accommodates in His person, in His spirit.

42

God sees a being of such likeness with His Son that there is no difference in the thought and mind of God when He considers this new creation called Man.

And remember that we have already discovered earlier that the New Creation is not new because of a time element attached to it. It is eternal, amen, in Him. We need to study that phrase: IN HIM. God wants us to discover all that is eternally ours IN HIM. IN HIM we live ...IN HIM we move ...IN HIM we have our being, amen!

I was meditating on that word *"associate"* and I found this definition in a dictionary. **It is occurring together in close union, so as to cohere in such a way that when any of them is afterwards presented to mind, the others are apt to be brought up in idea. That means that in God's thought, in God's associating Man in Christ, it would be impossible for God to bring to mind the thought of His Son and at the same time exclude Man. It means that it would be impossible for this God to think one single thought concerning His Son without promptly thinking, at the same time and on equal terms, of a being that exists in absolute association with His Son.**

I believe this thought to be so awesome that it is perhaps the most important thought penned down by Paul in all of the New Testament. I mean this thought alone is so awesome in its content and implication that it could stir and release all the appreciation and all the praise that Man as the recipient, the creature of God, could ever offer His Creator.

I am absolutely undone and overwhelmed as I am sitting here. My heart is burning within me and tears of joy and appreciation are running down my cheeks as I am experiencing God, His nearness, His fullness here in my spirit, just writing about these things. **Oh, the richness, the wealth of an association with Deity, that is so close, that neither time, history, nor contradiction could interfere in the mind of God to reduce His thought of Man, because He associated us in Christ before the ages. Before the foundation of the world, before the fall of Adam, before anything could happen in time, *that association existed as an eternal one, as a timeless one.***

The basis of this association forms the full foundation for our experience in the now, for our faith-expression in the life that we now live in the flesh. It is in the light of this association that the gospel reveals its truth *and finds its power.*

When Paul addressed that heathen audience in Athens as recorded in Acts Chapter Seventeen (and we have already briefly looked at that scripture), his confidence in addressing that audience stems from this understanding.

*"**Being then God's offspring**"* he says, Acts 17:29, *"We ought not to think that Deity has something to do with the art expression, or imagination of Man, that would liken Deity with something less than what Man himself contains and carries within his being."*

Paul continues there in Ephesians 1:4,

*"**He associated us IN HIM** before the foundation of the world, **that we should be holy and blameless before Him IN LOVE.**"*

God saw a being that stood **wrapped in His love!**

He saw a being that stood **holy and blameless in His love!**

*...**blameless**!*

You see, blame would immediately interfere with this association, with the enjoyment of it.

Any contrary evidence against this creature would immediately interfere with the quality of this association that existed from the beginning; *therefore God did not see a creature that would stand in a lesser position before God **than what His Son would stand in.**

Ephesians 1:5, *"He destined us, in love, to be His sons, through Jesus Christ, according to the purpose of His will..."*

In Chapter Three, verse Eleven Paul says,

*"This was according to **the eternal purpose,** which He has realized in Christ Jesus our Lord."*

God's eternal purpose found its full realization in Christ Jesus.

What is God's eternal purpose?

Chapter 4

God's Eternal Purpose

Let's go back to Ephesians 1:5.

God's eternal purpose is this: *"He destined us, in love, to be His sons, through Jesus Christ."*

In the light of this, where does the new creation find its origin?

We are created IN Christ Jesus.

When were we created? In the beginning when the *"LOGOS"* was, when the WORD was. We were conceived within the logic of God, within that conversation within Himself, within that conversation that took place within Deity, within that love fellowship within the Godhead.

"He destined us, in love, to be His sons, through Jesus Christ, according to the purpose of His will..."

We need to take a look at Isaiah 55 also and reflect and remind ourselves that the prophetic Scriptures reveal there that the purpose of God within His *"LOGOS"*, within His WORD, will prosper. God's purpose within His WORD, within His Son, and within His gospel, within His message to Man, will prosper!

And take note that His *"WORD"* referred to in that context there in Isaiah 55 *is not referred to as seed, but as the very* **moisture** *that comes and* **awakens the dormant seed that has been within the soil all along,** not just the seed buried *in the farmers field, but even the seed that has been dormant all along* **in the soil of the wilderness.**

I say again: His word, in that context is not referred to as seed, but as the moisture that awakens the seed **even within the wilderness.** So, the rain would come, with the full anticipation of an awakening, a response, to its moisture, so that instead of the thorn and the thistle (instead of the contradiction to this original association), would come up the cypress and the myrtle. If we want to fully comprehend and understand God's purpose and enter into the fullness of that purpose, of what is available to us in relationship with God, our Maker, our Father, we simply must begin to discover and see this reality that **God's eternal purpose existed in eternity.** *It has eternity behind it.*

Listen, the existence of the new creation is not the product or the fruit of a desperate attempt of God to somehow rescue the human race. It's not a light thought, it's not a sudden thought that occurred in the mind of God to just jump in and embark on an

experiment, to just experiment with Man. *Instead it is His eternal purpose.*

It is this eternal purpose of God that comes to us in the gospel; that comes to us like rain. And it is this gospel, this revelation, this rain, this knowledge of God's eternal purpose that surely prospers and could never disappoint.

Listen, the mind of God is secure. God is secure in this knowledge. His knowledge is not at risk. God's thought and eternal purpose is not fragile. God is not risking His thought when He communicates and entrusts His Word and His gospel to Man.

What if some are unfaithful?

What if some refuse to believe?

Wouldn't their unbelief threaten God?

Wouldn't their stubborn refusal to believe threaten His eternal purpose?

I mean wouldn't their unbelief disqualify God's faith?

Wouldn't Man's failure to be the recipient of such a thought prove God unfaithful?

"By no means!" says Paul, in Romans 3:3 & 4.

He says, *"Though all men be false, God remains faithful!"*

Listen, God's faith remains unchallenged! Uninterfered with! If there even is such a word? Ha... ha... ha...

It means: **It cannot be challenged. It cannot be interfered with. If all of mankind refused to believe what God knows to be the eternal truth about them, it wouldn't change what God knows to be the eternal truth about them. Even if all of mankind refused to believe, it wouldn't change anything! Truth is truth, amen! Our unbelief doesn't change the truth.** *It excludes us from enjoying what the truth affords us, but it cannot change the truth, amen.*

"We cannot do anything against the truth, only for the truth!" Paul says in 2 Corinthians 13:8.

Back to Ephesians 1:5,

*"He destined us, in love, to be His sons, through Jesus Christ, **according to the purpose of His will**..."*

This was *"...**for the purpose of His will**..."*

Ephesians 3:11 says,

*"...**This eternal purpose He has realized,** in Christ Jesus our Lord."*

And so in Christ Jesus Man now finds all the reference his faith needs, or ever will need, to correspond with. Let me say that again: **In Christ Jesus Man now finds total substance! The total substance of what his faith can function in. Because God has realized, He has expressed His eternal purpose in accurate definition in the WORD made flesh and standing face to face with Man as the audience of this word, of all that was revealed in Christ. In Christ God fully realized, fully revealed to all of Mankind His eternal purpose.**

Chapter 5

Praise of His Glorious Grace!

Ephesians 1:6 says,

"This is to the praise of His glorious grace!"

It is so wonderful to discover that the gospel does not demand faith, but it rather supplies and imparts faith!

Listen, anything that tries to talk you out of your completeness in Christ is another gospel.

The grace of God is such a marvelous thing! I am so glad to discover that God does not observe this universe and then decide which parts to love! No! Rather, He loved it into existence! And each and every moment it continues, it does so through the self-giving love of God. That is what grace is all about! Every moment you and I are alive, every moment we are still breathing, we are so by the grace of God, by the love of God. That is what the grace of God is. Grace is a gift!

Can you see how all this, this whole reality we exist in, how all of this is completely unnecessary because it is all pure grace?!

I mean it is so wonderful to discover that even though this whole universe is completely unnecessary, even though you and I are completely unnecessary, that even though there is no need or lack in God that could possibly motivate Him to create, *yet, He did so anyway, out of pure grace, <u>out of pure love</u>!*

Out of the overflow of creative *love*, proceeding from the God *who is love,* from the God who is too much, this whole universe was brought into existence, including you and I! We were brought into existence by the God who is too much, all because of pure grace! All because of love's desire!!!

I am so glad that God doesn't just put up with us. No! He desired us from the very beginning. He desires us still.

*"He destined us, **in love,** to be His sons, through Jesus Christ, **according to the purpose of His will**..."*

*"...**according to the purpose of His desire**..."*

*"...**according to His eternal purpose** ...**which He realized** ...in Christ Jesus our Lord."*

*"This is to the praise of **His glorious grace!**"*

This is where praise stems from. Praise is not some religious routine that we find ourselves

54

engaged in from Sunday to Sunday. No, **praise is the reflection of our spirit's appreciation of what our faith sees and knows in Christ to be true.**

"...to the praise of **His glorious grace which He _freely_ bestowed upon us** *...independent of Man's achievement* *..._freely_* *...independent of anything Man could offer in exchange..."*

You see, Man cannot buy favor from God! It is _freely_ bestowed upon the human race.

Together with the grace of life, this favor also is _freely_ bestowed upon the human race.

It is all bestowed upon us IN CHRIST JESUS.

This grace definition and this grace revelation of God's desire for us are _freely_ bestowed upon the human race. It was bestowed upon us IN CHRIST JESUS.

Grace was revealed and defined IN CHRIST JESUS.

The only requirement that qualifies the free bestowal of this grace is *the eternal purpose and desire of God realized.* That's it!

Ephesians 1:6,

"This was to the praise of His glorious grace, **which He _freely_ bestowed upon us _in the Beloved_."**

Listen, it is important for us to comprehend how God deals with Man. **God always deals with Man** ...**_in man._** For instance: In Abraham God spoke to Man. Romans 4:23 says there in the Scriptures where it was written about Abraham's faith that it was reckoned to him as his righteousness, it was not written or declared over him **_for his sake alone, but for us also._**

You see, faith taken on itself is rather empty, **_but the awareness of the oneness it beholds_** *is what faith is all about.* Abraham's faith was reckoned to him as his righteousness. This was not said about him for his sake alone, **but for us also.**

Thus God spoke to Man through Man, through a man, through a specific individual, *through Abraham.*

And so we also now find here in the New Testament that God deals with Man in Christ; in Jesus. Listen, **God deals with Man IN CHRIST. So, my only reference now is CHRIST. That is why the only word that can produce faith is CHRIST. The only word that can produce faith is when that word preaches Christ, when that word proclaims CHRIST.** Paul says, **_"I wanted to know_** *nothing among you, except Christ, and Him crucified!"*

It is interesting to note in James Chapter One, that when the word is preached ...which word? When Christ is preached, Man sees himself, as in a mirror. When God's eternal purpose is preached, when Christ is preached, when this gospel is preached, Man sees himself; he sees the very face of his birth IN CHRIST.

But let's get back to Ephesians.

Ephesians 1:6,

"...He freely bestowed this grace upon us IN THE BELOVED. In Him we..."

You see, where did **we** receive this grace?

IN CHRIST

Where did the new creation receive its origin?

Where did it receive its definition?

IN CHRIST

The new creation as a species exists for all eternity IN CHRIST. Man's association with that species, revealed in Christ, is an eternal association.

I want to encourage you to thoroughly follow the thought of what I am saying before you allow your mind to ask many questions and miss what is being said. Allow deep to call unto deep. Don't let any preconceived argument or idea hinder you from receiving what deep reveals unto deep.

Spirit combines with spirit.

"We impart this in words not taught by human wisdom, but taught by the Spirit, combining spirit with Spirit." - Paul says (1 Corinthians 2:13).

Chapter 6

We Have Redemption!

We are in Ephesians 1:7.

It says, *"**We have redemption**, through His blood..."*

Jesus manifested the new creation and re-birthed humanity when He stepped into human skin. John 1:14 echoes this; *"The Word became flesh and made His dwelling **IN us.**"* Not *"among"* us, as the NKJV puts it. The Greek literally says *IN US.* **Therefore, whatever happened to Him happened <u>to US</u>.**

Because of our eternal association with Him, realized in time, we were included IN HIM, in His life, in His death, burial, and resurrection. Thus, *"**We have redemption**, through His blood..."*

When we hear this good news, faith effortlessly pops up as a *"YES!"* to what He has done.

The word redemption literally means **to purchase back. To rescue out of the hands of. To buy back a slave in view to his freedom. To purchase and rescue. To**

bring someone back out of slavery and bondage.

But hey, listen now: Jesus did not come to rescue us out of the hands of God. Jesus did not come to save us from God, period. Because, *"**God was in Christ**, reconciling the world to himself."* **In Christ God made a personal appearance. He reconciled us to Himself.** There is no dysfunction in the Godhead. I say again: Jesus does not save you from God. Any message claiming He does *cannot be the gospel.*

I remember a little story we used in Africa, in my earlier days as a missionary going from village to village and ministering the gospel to scores of little kids in every village.

The story is about a little boy named Sippo.

Sippo made a little sail-boat and carved that boat himself with great skill and proudly engraved his name upon the bow of that boat, and he played with it and enjoyed it. He spent many hours playing with it and enjoying it until one dreadful day, when the river was in flood, he lost that little boat of his. That flood swept it away and he pined and cried for that little boat, wanting it and desiring it, longing for it to come back to him. Some weeks later, going to the pawn shop in town, he saw his little boat. *'It's mine!'* he exclaimed. He told the shop owner, *'Hey, that's my boat! I put myself into it; it's got my name on it. That boat carries my* inscription. I put my very being; my everything into it. I made it and carved it, from my heart, with my own hands! My identity is engraved upon its bow, and that little boat is engraved upon my heart! I desire it; *it is my boat!* And it was made to sail free upon the river, not to sit here locked up in your cabinet!'

But the owner said, *'You can't just have it back, if you want it you can buy it.'* You see, the just requirement of the law of economics and worth had to be fulfilled.

This little boy **could not enjoy his benefit from that little boat**, even though that little boat carried his name and his image: his very identity. Even though that little boat was his workmanship and his offspring, the fruit of his hands, the fruit of his very desire, he could not enjoy his benefit until he purchased it, until he fulfilled the just requirement of the law of economics, of worth and of value. He couldn't enjoy his benefit *until he redeemed it* and thus by that act of redemption, by that act of legitimate purchase, rescued it back out of the hands of the Pawn Shop owner. It once was lost, *but now it was found.* It was no longer for sale!

The scriptures very clearly reveal here in Ephesians 1:6 that, *"**IN HIM, we have redemption**..."* **He reveals and establishes our value and worth and thus secures the fact of our release. He in His person, as the eternal purpose of God realized, *secures***

61

our faith, and establishes God's faithfulness, so that even though any other man would fail to believe, yet God's faith and God's faithfulness will remain intact and unchallenged. Jesus is the eternal testimony of God's faith! Jesus is the eternal testimony of God's faithfulness!

And in Him, we, us, Mankind, were associated from the beginning, before the foundation of the earth. And the word *"foundation"* used there can also actually be translated, *"before the fall of the earth"* we were associated. Thus, before you got lost in Adam, **God already located you and found you in Christ!**

Listen, the beauty of the gospel is that **it reveals that the fall never broke the association. Man could not fall from God's love. Sin could not separate Man from the love of God,** *for "God so loved the world..."*

What attracted Him to the world? **His original thought and desire. His** *"logos"* **His original design attracted Him to the world. Likeness; deep calling unto deep. A sustained, eternal association** *in spite of the fall.* **He redeemed us, hallelujah! In our time calculation it was perhaps a little over two thousand years ago. But in terms of eternal reality, in terms of the WORD that was from the beginning,** *the Lamb was slain before the foundation of the earth!*

Listen, God built into His workmanship a guaranteed redemption. He built into your spirit an eternal spirit-witness. He made us compatible to Himself, to His Spirit. He made us in such a way that our spirits resonates when it hears truth, when it hears the gospel. We were custom designed to respond to redemption! A built in witness! And thus Redemption carries a guarantee that is not challenged in time. It does not fade or come to an end. It does not expire after 40,000 miles or two years ...or even after so many billions who transgress. It remains the truth, it remains valid throughout all generations!

Ephesians 1:6,

"IN HIM we have redemption, through his blood, the forgiveness of our trespasses, according to the riches of His grace."

I emphasize again: Do you know that Man's forgiveness is not measured by how Man responds to forgiveness? **It is measured by the richness of His grace!** Man's response is not the measure of God's grace. God's measure is **according to the richness of His grace, which He measured in His Son and which He then lavished upon us.**

How did God lavish grace upon us?

IN CHRIST!

How does God deal with the whole human race?

IN CHRIST!

God finds one individual and sees in this individual the whole human race. God does not exclude some. He includes all, in this one individual, JESUS CHRIST.

Chapter 7

From Glory to Glory!

Now Ephesians 1:9 says to us,

*"For He has made known to us, in all wisdom and insight, **the mystery** of His will, according to His purpose, which He has **set forth** in Christ."*

I remind you again of Ephesians 3:11 which say that, *"This purpose was **realized** in Christ."*

*"...He has **set forth, exhibited, His purpose, IN CHRIST.**"*

Now how are we drawn into this exhibition?

Through insight!

What did we see in Christ? What is the mystery revealed? What does Man see in Christ? What are we supposed to see?

We see ourselves there in Him! Man sees himself! I see myself!

You see, in Paul's preaching of the gospel, in 2 Corinthians 3:18 he says, *"Beholding the glory of the Lord, **as in a mirror,** we are transformed into His likeness."*

He says, *"...from glory to glory."* **His glory now becoming my glory!** And then he says in the next chapter as he continues that thought that, *"We commend ourselves to every person's conscience..."* And the word, *"conscience"* used there, means **joint knowledge.** *"So, I commend myself,"* he says, *"to every person's joint knowledge, anticipating the echo, the 'amen,' in my fellow Man."*

And we can be that bold because I know that if that person is born human, *then that's enough to qualify them to respond in joint knowledge.*

And then two verses later, in 2 Corinthians 4:5, Paul says, *"But we are not preaching ourselves."* Because, to many, who do not understand our message it sounds like; *'Hey man, these people are preaching themselves. They are exalting themselves too much! What they are saying sounds so arrogant!'*

But Paul responds by saying, *"Are we beginning to commend ourselves again?"* He says, *"**No**."* He says, *"**Listen, you are our letter of recommendation. Because something of what we said resonated with you it is therefore already engraved upon your spirit. Something is engraved upon your spirit that theology and tradition and error; that all of religion, all of man-made religious doctrine combined, cannot erase!"***

His likeness in your spirit cannot be erased!

Likeness cannot be erased!

Even if you just try it with animal species. Even if, through education, you can turn an Elephant into a circus creature, *you cannot erase its original design.* Perhaps you can change its conduct, *but you cannot erase its design.*

So Paul says, *"What we preach is not ourselves, but we preach **Him**, we are preaching **Christ**. We preach Christ, and Him crucified. We are preaching **HIM** in such a way **that you can see yourself** ...that you can see yourself **IN HIM** ...fully included IN HIM ...existing IN HIM ...living and moving and having your identity, your whole being IN HIM!"*

That, my friend, is the mystery revealed. We are preaching **Him** in such a way **that you can see your absolute union with Him.**

We are preaching **Him** in such a way **that you can see yourself there in Him, as in a mirror.**

We are preaching **Him** in such a way **that you can see yourself absolutely included in Him** ...we are preaching **His life** in such a way that you can see **your true design on display!** ...we are preaching **His death** in such a way that you can see **how effectively you died in Him!** ...we are preaching **His burial and His resurrection** in such a way that you can see **yourself raised there!** ...we are preaching

His ascension so that you can **fully see yourself ascended** with Him, **ascended already and having your life hidden with Christ in the bosom of the Father, seated there on His lap with Him!**

When did the new birth occur in time? You see, the new creation has its existence in eternity. It had its origin *from the beginning.* But when did it appear, when did that occur in time? 1 Peter 1:3 says that, *"We were born again **through the resurrection of Jesus."***

The reference to humanity's new birth is the resurrection of Jesus Christ. Christ's resurrection is the time realization of this eternal creature revealed again in the flesh!

So, in preaching Christ, in preaching His resurrection, I cannot but include Mankind.

Why?

Because Mankind was raised when He was raised! There is an eternal association between Christ and Man. When you and I bring to mind the thought of the resurrection, there is an inevitable association that occurs at the same time. I mean, when you mention the word *"resurrection"* to God, His thought cannot exclude Mankind being co-raised with Jesus.

Now Ephesians 1:9 says,

"For He has made known to us..."

Listen, God has not kept Man in the dark.

*"It is the same God who said, 'Let light shine out of darkness!', **who has also shone into our hearts**..."* - 2 Corinthians 4:6

He didn't even bother with our heads at that time, amen... ha... ha... ha. He short-circuited our heads **when He shone into our hearts,** amen... ha... ha... ha. *And our heads have been trying to catch up ever since!*

He shone **into our hearts,** *"...to give the light, of the knowledge of the glory of God in the face of Jesus Christ."*

He shone into our hearts **the light.** And what does that light equal?

*"...**the knowledge,** the understanding."*

What knowledge? The understanding of what?

*"...the understanding of the knowledge of **the glory of God** revealed..."*

Where was the glory **revealed** (that glory of God we lost in the Garden)? It was revealed, it was on display again, *"...**in the face of Jesus Christ.**"*

Just a few short verses before that, in 2 Corinthians 3:18 he says,

*"We all are now beholding the glory of the Lord **as in a mirror,** and as we do, we are transformed into His likeness!"*

Hallelujah!

Chapter 8

Fullness Revealed IN CHRIST!

Getting back to Ephesians 1:9,

*"For He has made known to us **in all wisdom
and spiritual understanding** (or insight)..."*

Not in a measure of wisdom, neither in a
measure of insight. No, *"...in <u>all</u> insight..."*

*"For He has made known to us **in <u>all</u> wisdom
and in <u>all</u> insight** (or spiritual
understanding), **the knowledge of His will**..."*

**The moment any doctrine or any definition
causes you to question and waver again in
your understanding, *drop it immediately!***

**Do not get attracted to and caught and
snared back into error, *into all the religious
error of your past!***

**Listen, you know what your faith knows.
So stay with it. I mean stay with what your
heart knows, *even if your head can't quite
figure it out and still argues with you,
amen!* Stay with what your heart knows!**

I mean, after all, we are dealing with a God that calls things that were not as though they were, *because they were.*

Listen; there is a reality to truth that is bigger than Man's understanding of it.

We all, you included, enjoyed much of what electricity could reveal and provide in terms of sight and sound, *before we had the faintest idea of how that electricity was ever generated.*

Don't be snared in technical definitions and disputes about words that will rob you of the fullness of your encounter and your enjoyment of the weight of the One who resides in you.

Ephesians 1:9,

*"For He has made known to us in **all** insight and wisdom the mystery of His will..."*

We are no longer dealing with a mystery amen, but we are seeing *as in a mirror,* <u>face to face</u>, amen.

*"For He has made known to us in all insight and wisdom the mystery of His will, according to His purpose which He has set forth in Christ as a plan **for the fullness of time.**"*

As far as God is concerned, time is measured by fullness. In Christ time has reached its fullness. All of time culminated in Him. Time has therefore lost its significance in terms of what it could add to what God has already revealed and done in Christ. Christ is therefore also the end of time because He is the fullness of time. He represents both the beginning of time and the end of time all at the same time, amen, because He is the fullness of time.

Listen; there is no greater event in time than the incarnation. It is the greatest event in all of time: *past, present or future.*

There can be no future event that will eclipse the incarnation.

That means that no future event will ever be a greater event, or of more significance than the incarnation.

Time itself cannot contain or reveal more than what its fullness reveals.

"In the fullness of time God sent forth His Son!"

Let's read Ephesians 1:9 again,

*"For He has made known to us, in all insight and wisdom, the mystery of His will, according to His purpose, which He has set forth in Christ, as a plan, **for the fullness of time.**"*

When all that God knew concerning His eternal thought of Man was realized in time, *time reached its fullness.* Time could not

possibly contain more of eternity than what it was able to reveal in this one new Man, in this one individual, Jesus Christ, *who represents fully this one new Man now, the new creation.*

Listen, how do you measure a glass of water? **You measure it in terms of fullness.** When is it full? **When that capacity can no longer contain more content.**

So therefore time's fullness was measured in Christ. Time's fullness can only be measured in Christ.

John 1:1,

"In the beginning was the Word, and the Word was with God, and the Word was nothing less than God..."

One translation says, *"...and that Word was face to face,* (or intimate) *with God, and the Word was God* (the fullness of God.) *...and that Word became flesh."*

Colossians 1:15 - 17 says,

"He (that Word which became flesh; that man: Jesus Christ) *is the very image of the invisible God, **the first-born of all creation,*** (the authentic original, the blueprint son)*; for in Him all things were created, in heaven and on earth, visible and invisible ...all things were created through Him and for Him. He is before all things, and in Him all things hold together..."*

74

It goes on to say in verse 18 - 20,

"...He is the beginning, the first born from the dead, that in everything He might be pre-eminent."

"For in Him all the fullness of God was pleased to dwell ...and through Him (God's purpose was) *to reconcile to Himself all things, whether on earth or in heaven, making peace by the blood of the cross."*

And so, what is the culmination of this fullness of time? I mean what does the fullness of time speak, what does it say? What does the fullness of time communicate with Man?

Ephesians 1:9,

*"For He has made known to us, in all insight and wisdom, the mystery of His will, according to His purpose, which He has set forth in Christ, as a plan, for the fullness of time ...**to unite all things in Him.**"*

"...IN HIM" ...**God's language is:** *"IN HIM."*

God's dealing with mankind is, *"IN HIM."*

*"...**to unite all things in Him.**"*

Hebrews 1:1-3 says, and I am reading to you from the Mirror Paraphrased Translation,

"Throughout ancient times God spoke in many fragments of thought and prophetic glimpses to

our fathers. But now, the sum-total of His conversation with Man has finally culminated in a son. He is the official heir of all things. He is, after all, the author of the ages. Jesus is what has been on the tip of the Father's tongue all along!"

The revelation of **Man's redeemed sonship**, as revealed in Jesus Christ, is the crescendo of God's conversation with humanity. Throughout the ages, God has whispered His name in disguise, to be revealed in the fullness of time, as the greatest surprise. **The exact image of God, His very likeness, the authentic, eternal thought, became voice and was made flesh in us.** The Composer of this concert masterpiece played out on the stage of life, knew that the notes scribbled on a page would finally find its voice in a symphony of instruments.

"We have our beginning and our being IN HIM (in Jesus). He is the force of the universe, sustaining everything that exists by His eternal utterance! Jesus is indeed the radiant and flawless expression of the person of God. He makes the glory ('DOXA', the **intent***) of God visible, and* **exemplifies the character, and every attribute of God, in human form***. (Genesis 1:26 & 27) This powerful, final utterance of God (the incarnation* **revealing our sonship***) is the vehicle that carries the weight of the universe. What He communicates is the central theme of everything that exists. The content of His*

message celebrates the fact that God took it upon Himself to successfully cleanse and acquit humankind. The man, Jesus, is now His right hand of power, the executive authority seated in the boundless measure of His majesty. He occupies the highest seat of dominion to endorse our innocence! His throne is established upon our innocence. ("...Having accomplished purification of sins, He sat down...")"

Ephesians 1:9,

*"For He has made known to us, in all insight and wisdom, the mystery of His will, according to His purpose, which He has set forth in Christ, as a plan for the fullness of time to unite all things in Him, **things in heaven and things in earth.**"* (RSV Translation)

Oh boy, there is just so much revelation in these Scriptures jumping off the page at me, and there is still so much I want to get to, but, let's quickly just read the rest of this context so we can carry on.

Ephesians 1:11,

"In Him (in Christ), ***we have obtained our inheritance** ...being predestined for this according to the purpose of Him **who accomplishes all things**...*"

Hallelujah!

God accomplishes, amen. God doesn't attempt and then fail. No, **He accomplishes.**

*"God accomplishes all things **according to the counsel of His own will**..."*

God's own will instructs Him.

I am so glad God doesn't have to ask around for everybody's opinions in order to come to some kind of compromised consensus! I am so glad God doesn't gamble with Man's destiny in such a way! God's own will instructs Him, *because He is the author of truth!* **Reality itself revolves around Him!**

Verse 12 says,

"We who first hoped in Christ..."

Why did we first hope, in this context?

Because we were the first to hear.

This Scripture could also be making reference to the prophetic word in the Old Covenant where Christ is referred to as the desire of the nations. *This is most likely the more accurate interpretation of this phrase used here in this passage.*

It could be read as saying: *"We hoped **first**..."* meaning: *"We hoped ...**from the beginning**."*

What was Man's hope from the beginning?

What was Man's hope?

CHRIST.

Thus, Ephesians 1:12 can be read this way,

*"The whole of Mankind ...hoped from the beginning in Christ, and that same Mankind who hoped in the coming Messiah, in the coming Christ ...we all, that same Mankind have been destined and appointed from the beginning **to live for the full expression of His glory.**"*

Our regular translations say,

*"...we have been appointed to live for the **praise** of His glory."*

But the very word *"praise"* used there indicates that, *"...we have been destined and appointed to live for **the full expression** of His glory!"*

Verse 13 says,

*"IN HIM **YOU ALSO**..."*

First Paul says, *"IN HIM **WE**..."*

Now he emphasizes and he says, *"IN HIM **YOU ALSO**..."*

*Listen, here IN CHRIST **we are all included!***

"Here IN CHRIST there can no longer be Jew, or Gentile, there is neither slave nor free, there

*is neither male nor female, there can be
neither Scythian or barbarian either, meaning
religious or non-religious or whatever, amen."*
          — Galatians 3:28 & Colossians 3:11

**Hey listen; when it comes to us preaching
the gospel *we are no longer addressing a
mixed audience.***

*"IN HIM **WE**..." "IN HIM **YOU ALSO**..."* That's
enough to send you off! That's enough to
commission you, amen!

Ephesians 1:13,

*"IN HIM **YOU ALSO**, who have heard **the
word of truth**..."*

The truth about what? The truth about our
redemption. The truth about our true identity.
The truth about our original design; *our true
design, **restored!*** The truth about our likeness
*...about being His image and likeness
exclusively.* The truth about the new creation
revealed, redeemed, and restored in Him. The
truth about *our reconciliation* to the Father.
The truth about *the gospel.* You have heard
**the gospel, the word of the truth, the gospel
of YOUR salvation!**

*"...**and have believed in Him,**"*

*"...and were sealed with the promised Holy
Spirit."*

Listen, the moment faith is quickened *through the hearing of the truth of who I really am,* the Holy Spirit takes effect and seals me. In my heart He seals what I've heard, He seals it in my heart as truth, He locks and seals and cements that truth into my spirit so that the human spirit can bear witness with the Holy Spirit *that we are indeed sons of God.*

Spirit with spirit combined, amen.

He who is joined to the Lord is one spirit with Him, amen.

For ages the human spirit remained confused about its true identity because of a foreign lordship, because of a foreign force that it was subjected to, *in hope.*

The moment of faith is the very moment of the Holy Spirit's sealing, *bearing witness with your spirit, amen.*

Verse 14 makes it clear that, *"He is Himself the guarantee of our inheritance ...so that we may acquire full possession of it..."*

"...to the praise of His glory!"

Meaning: *"...laying a hold of THAT for which I also was laid a hold of, in Christ ...the praise of His glory."*

And so, in the light of this, it is Paul's urgent desire that the believers will walk in insight, that the eyes of their understanding would be enlightened, **to know (to fully comprehend)** together with all the sanctified ones, **the full dimension, the full conclusion of what Christ reveals concerning them.**

Chapter 9

Stubborn Unbelief

The only thing that will continue to exclude Man from what this gospel reveals is ignorance and something called stubborn unbelief. It is interesting to note that even the word *"ignorance"* refers to **ignoring something that is apparent.**

In Romans Chapter One, Paul shows how apparent God is to Mankind. He says there that God has not left Himself without witness, but that God is on display in creation. He expresses that the very fabric of the visible cosmos appeals to reason. He says it clearly bears witness to the ever present sustaining power and intelligence of the invisible God, *leaving Man without any valid excuse to ignore Him.* He explains that what can be known about God is not only apparent in that which is made, but, he says, *'Day to day pours forth speech, night to night utters knowledge **so that no creature, not even us, the human race, has an excuse before God, our creator, to ignore Him.'***

He says there in Romans 1:19 that, even though Mankind has foolishly suppressed and concealed the truth in their unrighteousness, **God is not a stranger to them, *for what can***

83

be known of God is already manifest in them. God has revealed Himself *even within* **Man.** He is in their face.

Paul continues in Verse 21, and I am reading from the Mirror Bible again,

"Yet Man only knew Him in a philosophical, religious way, from a distance as it were, and failed to give Him credit as God. Their taking Him for granted and lack of gratitude veiled Him from them; they became absorbed in useless debates and discussions which further darkened their understanding about themselves."

He says in Verse 23 & 24,

"Their wise conclusions only proved folly. Losing sight of God made them lose sight of who they really were. In their calculation the true image and likeness of God became reduced to a corrupted and distorted pattern of themselves. Suddenly, Man has more in common with the creepy crawlies than with his original blue-print!"

The Message Translation puts it this way, *"So God said, in effect, 'If that's what you want, that's what you get.' It wasn't long before they were living in a pig-pen, smeared with filth, filthy inside and out."*

Verse 25 states,

"And all this because they traded the true God for a fake god, a figment of their own imagination, and worshiped the god they made up, instead of the God who made them - the God we bless, the God who blesses us. Oh, yes it's true!"

Verse 26 to 32 continues,

"And so worse followed. Refusing to know God, they soon didn't know how to be human either - women didn't know how to be women, men didn't know how to be men. Sexually confused, they abused and defiled one another, women with women, men with men - all lust, no love. And then they paid for it, oh, how they paid for it - emptied of God and love, godless and loveless wretches. Since they didn't bother to acknowledge God, God quit bothering them and let them run loose. And then all hell broke loose: rampant evil, grabbing and grasping, vicious backstabbing. They made life hell on earth with their envy, wanton killing, bickering, and cheating. Look at them: mean-spirited, venomous, fork-tongued God-bashers. Bullies, swaggerers, insufferable windbags! They keep inventing new ways of wrecking lives. They ditch their parents when they get in the way. Stupid, slimy, cruel, cold-blooded. But it's not as if they don't know better. They know perfectly well they're spitting in God's face. And they don't care, - worse, they hand out prizes to those who do the worst things best!"

Let's just continue reading there out of Romans 2 also, because there are no chapter breaks in Paul's original letter. I am still reading to you out of the Mirror Paraphrased Bible. In Romans 2:1-16 Paul is still addressing the depraved darkened mindset of Mankind. He says,

"Your presumed knowledge of that which is right or wrong does not qualify you to judge anyone. Especially if you do exactly the same stuff you notice other people do wrong. You effectively condemn yourself. No man is another man's judge."

He says,

"Yes I agree with your idea that God must judge all transgression, BUT your judging others does not make them any guiltier! God is totally impartial in His judgment; you are not scoring any points or disguising your own sins by telling on others!"

He then challenges our rotten thinking about God. He says in Verse 4,

"We cannot afford to get the wrong idea about God's goodness; the wealth of His benevolence and His stubborn refusal to let go of us in His love, His patient passion is to gently shepherd everyone into a radical change of heart."

He says,

"A calloused heart that resists change accumulates cause to self-destruction while God's righteous judgment (that fell on Christ) is revealed in broad daylight."

He continues,

"You calloused ones are on your own; your own deeds will judge you."

And listen to what he says here,

"Mankind's quest is to be constant in that which is good, glorious, and honorable, and of imperishable value. They are committed to pursue the original blueprint-life of the ages. Yet there are those who ignore the truth (about their identity as sons) through unbelief. They continue to exist as mere hirelings, motivated by a monthly wage (rather than sonship). **They believe in their failure and unrighteousness and are consumed by outbursts of anger and displeasure.** *Pressures from every side, like an overcrowded room (or a cramped foot in an undersized shoe) are the experience of the soul of everyone who does what is worthless. The fact that the Jews are Jewish does not make their experience of evil any different from that of the Greeks."*

He says in Verse 10,

"But in sharp contrast to this, bliss, self-worth and total tranquility is witnessed by everyone, both Jew and Greek, who finds expression in

87

that which is good. **We are tailor-made for good**.*"*

He continues, Verse 11,

"God does not judge people on face value."

He says,

"It should be obvious by now that ruin and self-destruction are the inevitable results of sin, whether someone knows the Law or not. Listen, righteousness is not a hear-say thing, it is law defined in practical living! For even a pagan's natural instinct will confirm the law to be present in his conscience even though he has never even heard about Jewish laws. Thus he proves to be a law unto himself. This proves that the Law is so much more than a mere written code, its presence in human conscience even in the absence of the written instruction is obvious, condemning or commending personal conduct."

Paul concludes in Verse 16. He says,

"Listen: every hidden, conflicting thought will be disclosed in the daylight of God's scrutiny, based on the good news of Jesus Christ that I proclaim. (The ineffectiveness of good intentions and self-discipline to produce lasting change will be exposed as worthless in contrast to the impact of the message of Christ's death and resurrection as representing mankind's death and new birth.)"

– Romans 1:18 to Romans 2:16 (Mirror Paraphrased Translation)

While we are in this vein of thought, let's get back to the book of Ephesians (4:17).

"Now this I affirm and testify in the Lord, that you must no longer live as the people of this world does..."

How do they live?

He says,

*"...**in the futility of their minds**..."*

He says,

*"They are darkened **in their understanding**..."*

Now Jesus once said that, *"...the eye is the lamp of the body. If the light that is in you is darkness, **how great is that darkness indeed.**"*

How can the light that is in you be darkness?

The term *"light"* refers to knowledge or understanding. Actually, it refers to more than that. It refers to the condition of your spirit. But it refers to knowledge and understanding here: *to the mindset you have; to your knowledge or supposed understanding about yourself and about others and about life and about God.*

*"...the eye is the lamp of the body. If the light that is in you is darkness, **how great is that darkness indeed.**"*

How can the light that is in you be darkness? When my spiritual eyes are not switched on. When my lamp does not reveal the light.

And so we see that *a darkened understanding* when it comes to spirit realities will cause Mankind to continue in their conduct *as if Jesus never was the revelation of their true design and identity.*

We are now speaking of the truth of the gospel, amen. Not Man's version of it, not Man's religious version of a watered down gospel that depends on how you interpret it, amen. We are not talking religion here, and we are not talking Man's various philosophies here. We are talking about the true gospel, *about the truth as God sees it, amen.*

The gospel is all about the truth of your design *as the Father knows you.* He revealed and restored that truth about you in Christ Jesus: *the truth of your design as the Father knows you.* So that you may now come to know Him as you have always been known. Not known since the day you put up your hand and said, *'I'm going to make a commitment to Jesus.'* No! Known as you have always been known *from the beginning, before Adam was.*

As I already said before: God already found you in Christ, way before you ever lost your way in Adam.

Ephesians 4:17,

"...do not be conformed to the people of this world in their thinking... (Religious or otherwise)*"*

Why?

"....because they are darkened in their understanding and thus alienated from the life of God..."

Because of What?

"...because of the ignorance that is in them, **due to their hardness of heart.***"*

James says in James 1:23-25,

"...they are like a man who sees the face of His birth, as in a mirror, but turns away (and rejects it, or puts no stock in it) *and straight away forgets* **what manner of man he is***..." ...Not what manner of man he could possibly be if he tries hard enough, no,* **he conveniently ignores what manner of man he IS.**

Because you see, in that mirror, in that word of truth, in that gospel of his salvation, *he heard the truth.* **What is it that he heard in that word of truth, the gospel of His salvation? I mean what did he see**

when that gospel came to him and held up God's eternal mirror in front of him?

James says that he is like a man who sees himself; *the face of his birth.* Not his natural birth, and not even his so-called, *'born again'* experience either. No. *He sees his original identity, his eternal design and origin; his birth in Christ.*

In the gospel what we are hearing is CHRIST, because we are not preaching ourselves and our own efforts and choices and decisions, we are preaching CHRIST. So, what you're hearing is CHRIST. But when you hear CHRIST *you're seeing yourself.*

And so, when you're hearing CHRIST how are you seeing yourself *then?*

Dead in His death, *dead to Adam and all that the fall represents.*

You are seeing yourself, buried in His grave, *that old identity inherited from Adam, inherited from your forefathers, inherited from your natural birth and identity was permanently buried and is now gone, done away with in His grave.*

When you are hearing CHRIST you see yourself resurrected in His life, *brought into newness of life in Him, restored to your original design.*

You are seeing yourself, seated in His glorious triumph, *completely reconciled and made one with the Father, in Him, in CHRIST, and restored to absolute authority over that old identity and that old life-expression, now living your life in union and absolute oneness with Daddy God, your true Father.*

Only a calloused heart that refuses to obey the truth, *to see the truth and fully embrace the truth,* <u>remains a prisoner of darkness</u>, *even though that person is already a forgiven and free individual.*

Why can we say this with such confidence and boldness?

Because we were not excluded. None of us were excluded when God associated Mankind in Christ Jesus from the beginning, even before the foundation of the earth ...and therefore neither were we excluded in His death, burial, resurrection, and ascension!

Let's just continue to read further here in Ephesians Chapter 4.

Remember Paul said,

"...do not be conformed to the people of this world in the way they think... (Religious or otherwise)*"*

Why?

Verse 19 says,

"...because they have become calloused and have given themselves up to licentiousness..."

The word *"licentiousness"* is a word which speaks of the **absence of restraint, reckless self-centered living, *which is dangerous and detrimental,* breaking out of and violating every good common sense safety restriction and barrier *without regard to the well-being of themselves or others.* It speaks of greediness, of an unbridled passion to practice every kind of uncleanness. It goes hand in hand with the concept of *destructive rebellion.* Thus, to live in licentiousness is to live *in self-destruct mode.***

What a contradiction to one who has been made in the image and likeness of God. What utterly depraved conduct in comparison to a holy, blameless innocence.

You were created in righteousness and true holiness: *in innocence, and for innocence,* amen!

Paul says,

"...the people of this world ...They have become calloused and have given themselves up to licentiousness..."

All because of what?

Ignorance! Hardness of Heart! Ignoring the truth! Refusing to believe and embrace the truth!

Listen, their unbelief will not disqualify God's faith and nullify it. Though every man be false, *we can do nothing against the truth!*

Listen, even though your religious definitions and your wrong conclusions, your definition of the truth, sometimes confuses you, *you can do nothing against the truth.* **The truth does not depend upon your definition.**

"You did not so learn Christ" - Verse 20.

In other words, Christ promotes the truth! Christ does not promote ignorance, hardness of heart, ignoring the truth, or refusing to believe and embrace the truth! Christ does not promote callousness and licentiousness, amen!

How did we learn Christ?

From Paul

Christ was preached **in such a way.**

Verse 20 & 21,

"You did not so learn Christ **Assuming that you have indeed heard about Him and were accurately taught in Him, as the truth is revealed in Jesus, and is on display in HIM."**

How does God deal with Man?

IN HIM!

How does God instruct Man?

IN CHRIST!

How was redemption sealed?

IN JESUS!

"...assuming that you have heard about Him, ***and were taught...”***

Were taught what?

*"...****and were taught IN HIM*** (the **IN HIM** realities) *...****just as the truth is revealed*** (**exactly as the truth is revealed**) *...****as it is*** ***accurately*** *revealed ...****in Jesus”***

Paul basically says that if you were taught about Him, *you should have been taught the right way.*

You should have been taught *the truth <u>as it really is</u>*.

That means you should have been taught the truth in a specific way. You should have been taught the truth <u>as it is IN HIM</u>, as it is revealed <u>IN HIM</u>. You should have been taught the IN HIM realities!

You should have been taught that IN HIM the truth was revealed accurately.

The truth was accurately revealed and openly displayed in Jesus! ...The truth of who the Father really is! ...The truth of who we really are: His offspring! His image and likeness! ...The truth of our original design! ...The truth of our true identity!

The true identity of both God and Man was revealed and on display there in Him!

Where does truth find its definition and authority?

IN JESUS!

Truth is not threatened even when Man becomes confused about its definition!

Truth's authority is secured and sealed for all eternity in one individual: IN CHRIST, in the man Christ Jesus; the original blueprint son of God, the first-born of the new creation!

Chapter 10

Put Off the Old Nature!

And now Paul says something, and I want you to see how logical his conclusion is based on what we have just looked at. His conclusion is not unreasonable or impossible, amen. It is logical, it makes perfect sense. It is not just a reasonable conclusion; it is the only correct conclusion. In fact, there can be no other conclusion, amen.

Paul concludes in Ephesians 4:22,

"Therefore, put off your old nature which belongs to your former manner of life (your old mindset, your old mentality, your old way of thinking, your old darkened understanding, your old supposed knowledge of yourself and of God and of others)."

Why, Paul, why?

Because that mindset, that mentality, that way of life, that lifestyle *was a lie, an utter deception!* That old way of thinking, that supposed understanding of yourself and of God and of your fellow Man was a lie, amen. It was a darkened understanding!

Why would we call it *a darkened understanding?* **Because it is a lie; it isn't the truth, amen!**

"...because it is corrupt ...it is influenced by deception, by a lie ...by deceitful lusts."

Then Paul says, in Ephesians 4:23,

"...and be renewed in the spirit of your minds..."

Paul basically echoes what he said back there in Verse 17, and what he said in Romans 12:2.

Let me quickly read to you Romans 12:2 also,

*"...**do not be conformed to the people of this world in the way they think** (religious or otherwise) **BUT RATHER, be transformed by the renewing of your mind.**"*

He continues here in verse 23 and 24 of Ephesians 4,

"...and be renewed in the spirit of your minds: put on the new nature," he says,

What nature?

The nature of your original design, the nature of the new creation, the nature of CHRIST, the Divine nature. Because you are God's offspring. You were made; you were brought forth in the image and likeness of God!

I have news for you: You are not here by accident! You are not here by the desire of your parents either! You are here by the desire of God!

"You were born, not of blood (not of mere natural origin) *nor of the will of the flesh, nor of the will of Man, but of God."* - John 1:13

The only reason why you exist is because God desired you! He loves you! You are more than your job description! You are more than all of your natural history combined can tell you about yourself! You are more than the sum total of all your experiences in the flesh, whether good or bad! You are a spirit-being who merely lives in a flesh and blood body! You are spirit. You are born of God, who is spirit! You merely live in this earth-suit, in this meat-box, in this flesh and blood body you call home. Peter said it is just a tent, a temporary dwelling place at best! - 2 Peter 1:13-16

Psalm 139 reveals the truth about you. It basically says,

"For you are awe inspiring and wonderfully made. God formed you and fashioned you, and then He placed you in your mother's womb, and there He clothed you with flesh!"

Hallelujah!

And now Paul says in Ephesians 4:23 & 24,

"...be renewed in the spirit of your minds: put on the new nature, which is made and brought forth after the true likeness of God, in righteousness and holiness."

Hallelujah!

But I want to get back to our discussion about a darkened understanding. There are still some things I want us to study and look at so we can clearly see it for what it is: *an absolute lie and deception!*

Paul said,

"Put off your old nature which belongs to your former manner of life, which is corrupt through deceitful lusts. Rather put on the new nature; be renewed in the spirit of your minds..."

He says,

"Rather put on the new nature by being renewed in the spirit of your minds..."

What keeps people imprisoned to darkness?

Ephesians 4:18 says, *"...**a darkened understanding does!**"*

And so, Paul's desire and petition before the Father, and his appeal to them (and us) *in writing this letter,* is to yield to the Father of our Lord Jesus Christ and to allow Him to help them understand and to bring them fully into what He has always desired for them, (and us).

His plea is: *"...that the Father of our Lord Jesus Christ will open your spiritual ears and your spiritual eyes, and give to you a spirit of wisdom and revelation, of insight and understanding, in the knowledge of Him."*

So that limited understanding would no longer rob them, or us, *of an unlimited experience!*

Why continue in darkness, practicing every kind of uncleanness that is born out of utter confusion and ignorance, *in total contradiction to the identity of the new species revealed:* the God-kind, *the companion of Deity?*

I mean, why continue in confusion and in ignorance and in darkness when it has been so clearly revealed that you are part of that new creation species?

Listen, the truth is: You also are a member of the household of Deity, *a child of God!* He is our origin. He fathered us, amen. He is our *"Abba"* our true Daddy, amen! We were made and brought forth out of God, in the very image and likeness of God, as the God-kind, to be the companion of Deity!

Hallelujah!

So, Paul says, *"...**be renewed in the spirit of your mind.**"*

That renewing of the mind is spoken of in the book of Colossians Chapter 3 in such an accurate way. He says in essence, there in Verse 1,

"If then you were indeed raised together with Christ Jesus, (**as a fact, as a realized reality**)*,"*

"Set your mind upon that."

Do not let your mind be influenced by a lie that does not confirm the truth!

*"**For you have died, and your life is hid with Christ in God.**"*

"Set your mind upon that."

Do not let your mind be influenced and ruled by a deception that refuses to conform to that truth!

*"**Put on the new nature, created after the likeness of God, in true righteousness and holiness.**"* This is what righteousness and holiness are all about; this is the truth about it.

"Therefore putting away falsehood, everyone speaking in line with truth to his neighbor..."

He says in verse 12 & 13,

*"Put on then, **as God's companions, holy and beloved,** put on compassion, kindness, lowliness, meekness, and patience, forbearing*

104

one another and, if anyone of you has a complaint against another, forgiving each other; as God has forgiven you, so you also should do..."

Hey listen this is what love is all about. This is the God kind of love. This is what the true likeness of God is all about. This is what the new creation looks like. This is what the God-kind looks like. This is what it means to put on the new nature, which is created according to God. This is what true righteousness and holiness is all about.

We can no longer do window-shopping when we read 1 Corinthians 13. This is not what we will eventually become gradually over time, after God somehow managed to chisel away the old nature! *What a lie we have been sold by religion!*

I say again, in 1 Corinthians 13 where Paul defines the love nature of the New Creation and of God, he is not speaking about what we may eventually grow into and become one day if we yield enough to God and if we are diligent enough, and try hard enough.

He is not talking about what we will become one day when we get to heaven. No listen; as you read 1 Corinthians 13 you are not doing window-shopping of what might could be one day. **You are actually looking in the mirror and seeing yourself:** *Your true design on display!*

God is love! *And so are you!*

You are love!

1 Corinthians 13 **defines who you are!** It defines who you are as a new creation, created in Christ Jesus for love, and good works (...which is an expression or the fruit of that love-nature), *because that is what God pre-designed you for and predestined for you to walk in.*

"Love is patient. Love is kind. Love is not jealous. Love is not prideful or boastful. Love is not arrogant. Love is not rude. Love does not insist on its own way. Love is not irritable. Love is not resentful. Love does not rejoice at wrong. Love rejoices in the right. Love bears all things. Love believes all things. Love hopes all things. Love endures all things. Love never fails. Love never ends."
- 1 Corinthians 13:4-8

Paul continues there in 1 Corinthians 13:10,

"When the perfect has come, the imperfect passes away."

And let me tell you, *the perfect has come.* You are perfectly revealed and placed on display as *"complete in Christ Jesus."*

"When I was a child," he says, *"I spoke like a child because I thought like a child. I reasoned like a child..."*

Paul says in 1 Corinthians 14:20, *"When it comes to evil, be as innocent as babes, but when it comes to the knowledge of who you really are revealed to be in Christ, be mature."*

He continues in 1 Corinthians 13:11,

"When I became a man, I gave up childish, immature ways."

He says,

"For now we see in a mirror dimly..."

He is talking about the time while we were still like little children in our thinking and reasoning, when we still weren't mature in our thinking, when we were living in a darkened understanding, when we were still ignorant about the knowledge of God and the knowledge of the new creation.

He says, *"...we saw ourselves dimly in a mirror..."*

There was no clear picture there. He is perfectly describing his former life under the Law, under religion and legalism and sin-consciousness and condemnation. We were looking in the wrong mirror, a mere shadow of the actual mirror, a mere shadow of the realities that were to come in Christ, *and have now come in the fullness of time.* **They have now fully been revealed.**

So, as a child, immature in our thinking and reasoning, *"we see in a mirror dimly..."*

*"...but then **face to face**..."*

Again, at the risk of being redundant, this *"then"* that Paul is referring to here is the *"...**now that faith has come!**"* **He is talking about the *"Now in Christ Jesus"* realities.**

We are no longer in window-shopping mode. We are no longer looking into a glass dimly. No, we are seeing the new man, we are seeing the new creation, we are seeing ourselves, our original and true design **face to face** in Christ Jesus.

Again he repeats himself and he says in verse 12,

"Now, (before faith came, before the truth came in Christ, while still living in the mindset and reasoning of a child concerning myself) *I know in part, but then* (once I understand the gospel; once I understand the truth revealed in Christ and in the work of redemption, THEN,) *I understand fully, even as I have always been fully understood."*

Chapter 11

Put On the New Nature!

We might as well go back to Colossians
Chapter 3 and read it through all the way to
Verse 17. But I want to read it to you out of the
Mirror Paraphrased Translation. It says it with
such simplicity, so clearly and beautifully, even
a child can grasp it.

No pun intended... ha... ha... ha...

Colossians 3:1-17,

Paul starts off with, *"You are in fact raised
together with Christ! Now ponder with
persuasion the consequence of your co-
inclusion in Him. Relocate yourself
mentally! Engage your thoughts with
throne room realities. His resurrection co-
raised you to the same position of authority
where you are now co-seated in the
executive authority of God's right hand."*

Verse 2,

*"Becoming affectionately acquainted with
these thoughts will keep you from being
distracted again by the earthly* (soul-ruled)
realm." (A renewed mind conquers the space

that was previously occupied by worthless pursuits and habits.)

He says,

*"**Your union with His death broke the association with that world; see yourselves located in a fortress where your life is hidden with Christ in God!** ("In that day you will know that I am in My Father, and you in Me, and I in you." [John 14:20] Occupy your mind with this new order of life; you died when Jesus died! That means that **whatever defined you before defines you no more!** CHRIST in Whom the fullness of Deity, the fullness of the Divine nature dwells, **defines you now! The secret of your life is your union with Christ in God!** [See Colossians 2:9 & 10.])*

*("Risen, then, with Christ, you must lift your thoughts above where Christ now sits at the right hand of God, you must be heavenly minded; not earthly minded, **you have undergone death, in His death, and your life is hidden away now with Christ in God.** Christ is your life. When he is made manifest, you are made manifest in his glory." - Knox Translation)*

Verse 4,

*"**The exact life on exhibit in Christ is now repeated in us. We are being co-revealed in the same bliss; we are joined in oneness with Him, just as His life reveals you, your***
110

life reveals Him!" (This verse was often translated to again delay the revelation of Christ to a future event! The word, ₁ **otan**, often translated as *"when"* is better translated as *"every time."* Thus, *"Every time Christ is revealed we are being co-revealed in the same glory* [in His glory]." According to Walter Bauer Lexicon, ₁ **otan** is often used when speaking of an action that is repeated. Paul declares our joint-glorification in Christ! We are co-revealed in the same bliss. [See 1 Corinthians 2:7-8, Romans 3:23-24, Romans 8:30, 2 Peter 1:3.] **In Him we live and move and have our being; in us He lives and moves and has His being!** [Acts 17:28])

Verse 5,

"Consider the members of your body as dead and buried towards everything related to the porn industry, sensual uncleanness, longing for forbidden things, lust and greed, which are just another form of idol worship." (Idol worship is worshiping a distorted image in your mind, really, a distorted image of yourself!)

"These distorted expressions are in total contradiction to God's design and desire for your life." (The sentence, *"upon the sons of disobedience or the sons of unbelief"* was added later in some manuscripts.)

He says in Verse 7,

"We were all once swept along into a lifestyle of lust and greed."

Verse 8,

"<u>But now</u>, because you realize that you co-died and were co-raised together with Christ, you can flush your thoughts with truth! Permanently put these things behind you: Things such as violent outbursts of rage, depression, all manner of wickedness, slander (any attempt to belittle someone else and to cause someone to receive a bad reputation, [**blasphemos**], *and every form of irregular conversation."* (The lifelong association with sin is broken. **The dominion of the character of God is revealed again in ordinary life.**)

"That old life was a lie, foreign to our design! Those garments of disguise are now thoroughly stripped off of us in our understanding of our union with Christ in His death and resurrection. We are no longer obliged to live under the identity and rule of the robes we wore before, neither are we cheating anyone through false pretensions. (The garments an actor would wear define his part in the play, *but cannot define him.*)

"Now we stand fully identified in the new creation, renewed in knowledge, according to the pattern of the exact image of our Creator."

"The revelation of Christ in us gives identity to the individual, beyond anything anyone could ever be as a Greek or a Jew, American or African, foreigner or famous, male or female, king or pawn. From now on everyone is defined by CHRIST; everyone is represented in Christ. (In seeing Him, not just recorded in history, but revealed in us, we discover the face of our birth as in a mirror! [James 1:18])

Verse 9,

"You are the product of God's love; He restored you to His original thought. You belong to Him exclusively. It is like changing garments. Now that you have gotten rid of the old, clothe yourself with inner compassion, kindness, humility, gentleness, and patience, (Just like you were once identified by your apparel, the characteristics of these qualities define you now.)

"...upholding one another in positive expectation. If anyone finds fault with another, restore that person to favor, remembering how the Lord's forgiveness has transformed our lives."

He says in Verse 14,

"Wear love like a uniform; this is what completes the picture of our oneness."

"Appoint the peace of Christ as umpire in your hearts. We are all identified in the same person; there is only one body. We are born to be a blessing and exhibit His benevolence."

Then in verse 16 & 17 Paul concludes with this,

"CHRIST is the language of God's logic. Let His message sink into you with unlimited vocabulary, taking wisdom to its most complete conclusion. This makes your fellowship an environment of instruction in an atmosphere of music. Every lesson is a reminder, echoing in every song you sing, whether it be a psalm (raving about God in praise and worship accompanied by musical instruments) *or a hymn* (a testimony song) *or a song in the spirit* (a new spontaneous prophetic song). *Grace fuels your heart with inspired music to the Lord."*

"Your every conversation and the detail of your daily conduct reflect Him. His name and lordship defines your lives and inspire your deep gratitude to God the Father for His grace."

Then he says, *"His peace is the umpire of your every relationship, especially in the family!"*

Chapter 12

Raised to Newness of Life
IN HIM!

But let's get back to Ephesians. There are a few more things I want to share with you concerning our theme of the origin and the manifestation of the new creation.

Ephesians 2:1 & 2,

"And you, when you were dead through the trespasses and sins in which you once walked, following the course of this world, following the prince of the power of the air, the spirit that is now at work in the sons of disobedience..."

What do they fail to obey?

They fail to obey the truth. They are hearers of the word, but they refuse to look deeply into the perfect law of liberty, and thus they forget what manner of man they are, so they fail to obey the truth.

Paul says in verse 3,

"Among these we all once lived in the passions of our flesh, following the desires of body and mind, so we were by nature children of wrath, like the rest of Mankind."

Mankind, the offspring of God, exhibiting the nature of the enemy in their conduct *all because of one reason:* **Darkened understanding, strongholds in their thinking, ideas and beliefs, mindsets and thought processes that refuse to obey the truth.**

This brings us to question, was it possible to obey the truth *before Jesus?*

Was it possible to obey the truth before the *"logos"* was revealed in the flesh?

Absolutely!

Why?

Because the Word, the *"logos"* was from the beginning! Otherwise Enoch and every other man of God who revealed faith wouldn't have stood a chance to even consider relating to Deity. (You should go read my book, *"Reigning in Righteousness"* if you want to explore these thoughts some more.)

If the fall of Man so excluded them from the word of truth, from the word of His grace, then God might as well forget about getting any response from a man who has so taken upon himself the likeness of the enemy that there is no possible reflection of anything Divine left in that man, of a longing to again be restored to God.

Ephesians 2:4 & 5,

*"But God, who is rich in mercy, **out of the great love with which He loved us,** even when we were dead through our trespasses, made us alive together with Christ* (by grace you have been saved)..."

When did He make us alive together with Christ Jesus? **While we were still dead in our trespasses!**

Listen, God made Mankind alive before Mankind believed. He brought us into newness of life together with Christ Jesus!

Thus the new birth of this new creation occurred before you were! By grace you have been saved!

Verse 6,

*"...and He raised us up with Him, and made us sit with him in the heavenly places ...**in Christ Jesus*** (It all happened in Christ Jesus)..."

Verse 7,

"...so that in all the coming ages He might show (to us and through us) *the immeasurable riches of His grace in His kindness towards us* (demonstrated and exhibited) *there in Christ Jesus."*

Verse 8,

"For by grace you have been saved through God's faith. This is not your own doing, it is the gift of God."

Verse 9 says,

"It is not based on our works, lest any man should boast."

"FOR we are His workmanship *...***created in Christ Jesus** *...***for love***..."*

I wish we could just stop and camp at every sentence, because every sentence is chock and block full of the love of God for us! Every word is so rich and so full, so jam-packed full of the love and the goodness and the kindness of God in His grace towards us! But let's just get to our theme.

Chapter 13

Created IN CHRIST JESUS!

Ephesians 2:10 continues,

*"FOR we are His workmanship, created in
Christ Jesus for love, and for good works*
(Note: These *good works* are the fruit of the
impact of that love-affair upon our hearts; it's
the natural outflow of love.) *God prepared us
beforehand for this, so that we should walk in
it."*

Where did God create Mankind?

In Christ Jesus

Let's just read Ephesians 2:12 quickly,

*"Now remember that you were at that time
separated from Christ..."*

What separated Man from Christ?

The fall of Adam did. *Ignorance did!*

Paul agrees, he says,

*"...you were alienated from the commonwealth
of Israel; you were strangers to the covenants
of promise..."*

In other words, **you were ignorant. You knew nothing about these things, and even if you did, they weren't for you, or so you were told and so you understood. You were left outside in the cold; you were left with a darkened understanding!**

He says,

"...having no hope and without God in the world."

These are the same Gentile people, remember, the ones Paul addressed there in Athens in Acts 17, *who have their life and their being in God.* **But they are still without Him, not enjoying His intimate embrace due to** *the ignorance that is in them.*

Just like that little boat, in that cold shop, still carrying the imprint of its designer. It was the property of its designer, it was even desired by its designer and maker, but it was separated from him and from enjoying the life it was designed for in the friendship and companionship of its maker.

Ephesians 2:13,

*"**But now** in Christ Jesus (in the fullness of time)..."*

Can we conclude together that this *"**But now**,"* refers to the fullness of time?! I mean, is there a link between NOW and the fullness of time we have looked at in Chapter One?

God's eternal purpose found its full expression in one man!

*"BUT NOW IN CHRIST JESUS <u>you</u> who once were far off, **have been brought near in the blood of Christ.**"*

Can you see how this association between you and Christ Jesus from before time began comes into play again and again!

When you bring up the name of Jesus, God the father of us all, cannot help but think of you!

"For He is our peace."

(Romans 5:1 *"Now we have peace with God through our Lord Jesus Christ, being justified by God's faith!"*)

Paul says, *"**For He is our peace!**"*

Amen!

He is our healing. He is our identity. He is our everything. He is our peace.

"He has made us both one, and has broken down the dividing wall of hostility by abolishing in His flesh the law of commandments and ordinances so that He might create in Himself..."

Where are we created?

In Christ Jesus!

So that He who sanctifies and those who are sanctified are fully associated, because they share the same origin, both in God, and now in the incarnation and in the resurrection!

*"He has made us both one, and has broken down the dividing wall of hostility by abolishing in His flesh the law of commandments and ordinances, **so that He might create in Himself <u>one new man</u>** ...in the place of the two ...thus making peace. He reconciled us both to God, in one body, through the cross ...thereby for all practical intents and purposes, bringing the hostility to an end."*

When you look at humanity you are looking at one kind. The two no longer exist. The Jew versus the Gentile ceases to exist in this *"one new man".*

Who are reconciled?

The religious people? Or both the religious and non-religious people? Or maybe just us the believers? *Or <u>ALL</u>?*

BOTH, amen! <u>ALL</u> of us!

What keeps some from enjoying the one new man, the new creation? **Darkened understanding.**

122

"If the light that is in you remains dark, unenlightened, how great is that darkness indeed." - Matthew 6:23

"While you have the light, believe in the light, that you might become sons of the light!" - John 12:36

"The eye is the lamp of the body." - Luke 11:34

What do you see? Do you see what the Father sees in Christ?

"Here there cannot be Jew and Gentile, but CHRIST is all ...and in all." - Colossians 3:11

I remind you again of Ephesians 1:10,

"As a plan for the fullness of time, to unite all things in Him, the things in heaven and the things on the earth."

God does not exclude any! *Full insight reveals full inclusion!*

"...He has reconciled us both to God in one body through the cross, bringing all hostility to an end." - Ephesians 2:16

Through the death of the cross Humanity died in His death. Through the death of the cross the Gentile world died in His death. As far is God is concerned it has been totally undone. It stopped existing!

Through the death of the cross the Jewish nation also died in His death. As far as God is concerned the Jewish nation came to an end. The Jewish nationality was done away with!

*"...**He has reconciled us ALL to God in one body through the cross** ...thereby bringing all hostility to an end."*

Hostility was brought to an end!

"And He came and preached peace..."

Hallelujah!

"He came and proclaimed peace..."

Why?

Because ALL hostility has been brought to an end when He revealed that we have IN ALL REALITY no other identity other than our identity revealed in Him!

He revealed that we are ALL IMMEDIATE FAMILY of one another ...because WE ARE ALL CHILDREN OF GOD; MEMBERS OF HIS HOUSEHOLD ...*IMMEDIATE FAMILY!*

Why is that so difficult to understand? It is not too difficult to understand, amen!

When hostility comes to an end, peace may be proclaimed! Not as a possibility, but as

a reality! Not as something to be attained to through compromise, but *as a reality!*

"He came and proclaimed peace to you who were far off..."

You see, they may have been Gentiles by birth and had no share in the commonwealth of Israel. They may have been born outside of the promise, outside of the covenant. *"**BUT NOW**,"* Paul says, *"**YOU have been brought near!**" "**He came and proclaimed peace to you who were far off** ...and to those who were near."*

Who were they? Who were those who were near? **The Jews. They were supposed to be so close to God, being a covenant people and all. BUT NOW THE SAME GOSPEL IS PREACHED TO BOTH. I mean, the same peace is now proclaimed to both!** *For in Him there is no more Jew, or Gentile. That has all been done away with!*

When we find out that there is only one human race, one new man, as far as God is concerned, that we are all family, when we find out we are all children of God, when we find out we are all immediate members of His household and that we have everything in common, then everything that separates us falls away and all hostility comes to an end!

God no longer recognizes or acknowledges any nation whatsoever. And get this: Not

even the current nation of Israel, not even the present day Jewish Nation. He only recognizes and acknowledges His own peculiar people, a royal priesthood, His new holy nation, His only holy nation, the one new man, the new creation!

"Neither circumcision, nor the lack of it avails anything, <u>only the new creation</u>."
— Galatians 6:15 & Galatians 5:6

Why even bring up the subject of circumcision, or the lack of it, Paul? **Because you see, circumcision in this instance is a reference to the identity of the Jews, to their national identity as the nation of Israel.**

There is no more Jew, *nor Gentile*. That means there is no more England, or France, or South Africa, or Russia, or China. For as far as God is concerned *none of this stuff matters anymore.* There is no United States of America, or the nation of Israel either. There is only CHRIST. CHRIST is all that exists. CHRIST is all that is left. As far as God is concerned, *"<u>CHRIST is all</u> ...and in all!"* - Colossians 3:11

Only the New Creation is of any consequence! There is no more Jew, nor Gentile! *Every natural and national identity, every cultural identity we cling to is a lie, a deception! There is only one identity that matters, only one identity that is of any*

consequence whatsoever: "CHRIST IS ALL ...and in us all!" - Colossians 3:11

"For in Him we both have access in one spirit to the father of us all." - Ephesians 2:18

Therefore Paul concludes in verse 19,

"You are no longer strangers and sojourners or foreigners, but you are all (both Jew and Gentile) *fellow citizens together with all the sanctified ones worldwide* (from every tribe, tongue, and nationality) *and across all of time; members of the very household of God."*

What would cause Man to uphold what doesn't exist as far as God is concerned? What would cause Man to uphold that which doesn't have any significance anymore? What would cause Man to uphold his nationality and his patriotism, his natural identity as a Jew, or as an American, or as a South African for that matter? What would keep Man submitting to an inferior identity, an inferior sense of self? What would keep Man submitting to *a darkened understanding*?

Refusing to believe the truth of the gospel! Refusing to believe what manner of Man he really is!

Paul says,

"You are no longer strangers and sojourners and foreigners..."

"BUT you are fellow citizens; members of the very household of God..." - Ephesians 2:19

You Gentile world, you are included! Your identity has been redefined! The mystery has been revealed: You are all fellow citizens! As close to being a citizen as you can possibly get; *even closer.* You are members of God's family, not extended family, NO! *Immediate family!* You are members of the very household of God! That's who you are! That's your new identity! Your true identity! *Your only identity!*

On what basis?

On the basis of your origin in God. On the basis of the fact that you are a spirit-being merely living temporarily in a flesh and blood body! And on the basis of the new creation, on the basis of this one new man, of this one new identity that has now been created by God Himself.

"All the kingdoms of this world, they have now become the kingdom of our Lord and of His CHRIST!" - Revelation 11:15

The little stone, according to the book of Daniel, that Rock, was cut out from heaven by no human hand and struck that rigid statue that we have erected, that monument to ourselves, that substitute, man-made self-image and identity with its glorious head of golden glitter
128

and its silvery bust and bronze body, that egotistical false image of vanity and piety. That little stone, that Rock, struck it on its feet of iron and clay and ground it to powder, and God's winds of change that came in the fullness of time blew it away! In its place, that little stone grew in men's minds, in its identity as the Rock of ages, and it now fills the whole earth! He has become and always has been the true image and likeness of God, restored and revealed again and again in ordinary human life! (See Daniel 2:32-35)

Listen, we are not speaking about Man's response right now; or his need to, so don't let that thought mess with your head right now and interrupt and interfere with our discovery here in these Scriptures. We are not speaking of Man's response, or about what Man is going to do with what God has done and with what God have revealed. We are dealing right now with what actually happened. We are speaking about the eternal, unchanging truth behind the gospel.

Paul says in Ephesians 2:19,

"You are all immediate members of the household of God..."

"That household and that identity is built, it's restored, upon the foundation of the apostles and prophets..."

Amen!

Because they all proclaimed this, from Moses to Isaiah to Paul, they all proclaimed this! Even Jesus proclaimed this, amen. He was the most vocal proponent of these things, amen!

*"**Christ Jesus Himself being the chief cornerstone,** IN WHOM the whole structure is joined together as a holy temple in the Lord; IN WHOM YOU ALSO are built into this structure, this belief-system, this identity, this persuasion in the truth of the gospel, to be a dwelling place of God in the Spirit."* - Ephesians 2:20-22.

*"You who pursue righteousness, **look to the rock from which you were hewn.**"* - Isaiah 51:1

You were cut in that quarry! You were created in Him!

In Colossians 4:4 Paul says,

"My sincere desire is that my message will accurately unveil the mystery of Christ in its most complete context: YOU! This is the mission of my life!"

Listen, God is not seeking to somehow squeeze you into a place you don't quite fit or don't belong.

1 Kings 6:7 reveals that. It says,

"In the day when the temple of the Lord was built during the days of King Solomon, it was with stone prepared at the quarry; so that neither hammer nor axe nor any tool of iron was heard in the temple, while it was being built." **Because every stone was cut to size, to perfection, in the quarry!**

Where were you created?

Where were you cut to perfection?

IN CHRIST JESUS! In that eternal association with HIM in the beginning! And therefore the fullness of time also reveals as an eternal testimony that same reality: **your full inclusion and your full identity!**

1 Peter 2:4-10 also unveils and confirms the prophetic significance of that picture there in 1 Kings 6:7 as Peter speaks in Verse 5 of the fact that, just as with the temple of old, *you too, like living stones, are being built into a structure, into a specific predefined identity, to form a spiritual house, a temple, **a dwelling place of God** in the spirit.*

He says,

"You are God's chosen race, a royal priesthood, a holy nation, a people revealed to be His own possession..."

Peter says,

*"You are a people set apart for His own possession, so that you may proclaim the excellencies of Him **who called you out of darkness into His marvelous light!**"*

He says,

"Once you were not a people, but now you are revealed to be God's people..."

...And so you have become God's people indeed!

Hallelujah!

Some of you may wonder, *'If all are included in Christ's work, what is the point of preaching the gospel to people?'*

In the parable that Jesus told of the prodigal son, that son who lost his way *was always loved by the father and always remained a son, even when he ran away and even when he lived like hell!*

You see the father only ever deeply desired his son to come home and enjoy their relationship again.

Listen, God was in Christ, reconciling the whole world to Himself and now longs that every person would awaken to that reality and enjoy their Father!

This is exactly why Jesus went from town to town announcing to the people and

challenging them to, *"Change the way you are currently thinking because I declare to you that heaven is already here! It is right here in the here and now!"*

He was not preaching and saying, *'Heaven will be here some day!'* or, *'Here's how you can go to heaven when you die.'*

No! He said: *"Heaven is at hand!"*

This should be our simple message to people: Today, right now, trust that Jesus has forgiven you, loved you always, and loves you still, and that He made a way for you to experience true life! Heaven is here! It is now! It is your portion!

Chapter 14

The Stewardship of God's Grace-Message!

This is why Paul continues in Ephesians Chapter Three,

*"**For this reason**..."*

Was there reason in Paul's appeal? Was there a reason for him doing what he was doing?

"For this reason, I, Paul, a prisoner of Christ Jesus (imprisoned by this truth; by the largeness, by the scope of this truth. He says, 'I'm a container, I contain this truth') **on behalf of you Gentiles**..."*

Who is Paul's audience here in Ephesians?

The Gentiles. Those who were far off! It's the same audience he had in Acts 17. He fully identified with them. Revealing to them that, 'There is no difference between you and I, except for ignorance maybe, stubborn unbelief maybe, but as far as God is concerned there is no difference between us, between you and I.'

"...in Him <u>we</u> live and move and have our being..." - Acts 17:28

He says to them,

*"**Seeing then that <u>we</u> <u>are</u> the offspring of God**..."* - Acts 17:29

He says,

*"...**we ought not to think, this, that, and the other thing**..."*

He says,

*"...**we are indeed His offspring!**"*

"...assuming that you have heard," Ephesians 3:2, *"...of the stewardship of the grace of God that was given to me **for you**..."*

You see, the Gentiles, the idol worshiping masses, the ignorant masses can so easily be misled and interfered with in their understanding and in their faith, by the forces of religion and man-made philosophy. **And so Paul makes His concern the very hearts and minds of these Gentiles.**

He explains to them in verse 3,

"...how the mystery was made known to me by revelation from God (by insight and understanding given to me by God), *as I have written briefly."*

He says,

"When you read this, you can also fully perceive what I perceive; you can perceive my insight into the mystery of Christ."

Paul continues in Verse 5,

"This mystery was not made known to the sons of men in other generations before us in the depth that it has now been revealed to us, His holy apostles and prophets, by the Spirit."

Why?

Because of ignorance, because the fullness of time had not yet come.

You see, Paul explains in Acts 17 that before the fullness of time, *during the time of ignorance,* they were still living a life trapped within the boundaries of time and location, within the boundaries of their national identity and their nation's borders.

But God had hoped all along that even in that setting, even within those boundaries, they might recognize the call within their hearts. He had a hope that they might recognize their true design crying for release and that they might begin to seek, they might grope around in the dark and feel after God, in order to find Him and know Him and come to know themselves as they have always been known by Him. *Thus, they would escape the limitations and boundaries of a lesser, inferior expression of life. They would escape a life*

in the flesh, a life lived trapped in a mere human existence and struggle for survival.

And I am paraphrasing now, but you knew that already. Listen, I am not twisting the Scriptures or trying to take away from the Scriptures, I am merely expounding and explaining, so that what is actually being said will become clear to you. So don't shut me down, okay?! Relax Max and enjoy the ride! Ha... ha... ha...

Verse 6,

*"This is the mystery: The Gentiles, the idol worshiping masses, the ignorant masses, **are also fellow heirs, members of the same body, members of Christ, and partakers of the promise in Christ Jesus,** that very promise that was fulfilled through the gospel, through that work of redemption accomplished in Christ Jesus, in which we were all included."*

He says,

*"This is the mystery: The Gentiles are fellow heirs; **they are also included!**"*

How can we reason theologically, if you want to put it that way; doctrinally, **how Gentiles; unbelievers and outsiders, could be considered fellow heirs? I mean, they had not even heard! They had not even responded! They had not even repented, but they are already considered fellow heirs.**

138

Why?

Because of one new creation ...because of one man, who reconciled both!

Paul says,

"They are members of the same body, (not excluded in other words.) ...Partakers of the promise in Christ!"

He continues, and He says that,

"Now, through the gospel, through hearing and believing the gospel, the Gentiles may also now partake of that which was fulfilled and accomplished in Christ!"

Paul says in verse 7,

"Of this gospel, of this good news, I was made a minister."

"This gospel, and my being a minister of it, is concerning the gift of God's grace."

"This understanding, this revelation, this gospel, this insight into the gift of God's grace was given me by the working of God's power; by the very working of that grace within me."

Paul says,

"Yes, even to me, though I might be considered by some to be the very least of all the saints..."

[Paul trusts his experience of God, and of Christ, *over his own upbringing,* over the opinion of his former colleagues, the Pharisees ...even over the opinions and teaching of the other Twelve Apostles, even over Peter's opinions, and over the opinions of the Jewish Christians. Paul doesn't follow the expected sources of outer authority in his life, neither his own Jewish religion nor the new Christian leaders in Jerusalem. He dares to listen to, *and trust,* his own inner experience, which trumps both of these establishments.

It's amazing, really, that today, our religious institutions makes him the hero that it does, and almost half of the New Testament they compiled is attributed to him, **because in many ways he is an outright rebel and would be shunned and thrown out of those very same institutions if he were around today.**

He was not by any definition a *"company man".* He was not any body's **company in fact!** In terms of human biographies, he is almost in a category all his own. It is ironic that the ability to trust one's own experience to that degree has not been affirmed later by the church, even till this very day, **even though both Jesus and Paul did exactly that. They trusted their experience of God, and of the Christ in them, *in spite of the dominant tradition.***

And yet the church came along and over time domesticated both Jesus and Paul. We were never told to trust our own experience. (Yet the Church still produced people like Augustine, Francis, Teresa of Ávila, Thérèse of Lisieux, and Teresa of Calcutta, **who trusted their own soul experience against the tide.**

Once you know something, you can't deny that you know it. You don't need to dismiss outer authority. Its intuitions are often correct, *but you're not on bended knee before it either.* The church's fear of inner authority has not served the Gospel well and has not served history well either. I am afraid this has to do with those in charge wanting to keep you co-dependent. *I don't think Paul wants to keep you dependent upon him at all.* **He is the great apostle of freedom; *a scary freedom that much of tradition, and most clergy, have not been comfortable with at all.*** - Richard Rohr (Galatians 5:1-12, Romans 8:20-23)].

So you might think, *'What does this Paul fellow have to say? After all, he doesn't come through our school and we have heard some pretty disturbing rumors about him. He was in isolation too long, in rebellion you know. That independent spirit in Paul just kept him out there in the wilderness for thirteen years at least. What a rebel he was, refusing to submit to the traditions of Jerusalem, the wonderful comfort-zone. **I mean, what would a lesser apostle like Paul really know?**'*

Only this: That in Him we may be nothing, a nobody in the eyes of men, *but we need nothing either.* We are not commended by Man. We are not recognized and schooled by human institution, **so that God can display us perfect by His grace.** God called us and chose us by His Spirit of grace, **so that in the weakness of man, the strength and the power and the wisdom of God, not impeded by human opinion, might be revealed** *to make all people see.*

What are we called to do? **We are called to make all people see!**

It is the lack of insight that separates Man from God. Not as far as God is concerned, of course, *but certainly as far as that individual's experience is concerned.*

The lack of insight separates Man from what he really is: Forgiven. Healed. Restored. Reconciled. Blameless. Holy!

But the opposite is also true, then, and that is that insight unites and joins Man with God, and with what and who that Man really is.

Hallelujah!

Jesus came, not to get us to focus on our sin, *but to focus on the greater truth about us.*

He came to reveal that, *"What is true in Him is equally true in You!"*

He came to reveal your original innocence by introducing you to your true self, *fully redeemed and fully restored!*

What is in Him is in you, absolutely, therefore; that which is in you exactly matches that which is in Him!

Religion always excludes people. In fact the very word *'Pharisee'* means **separatist.**

Jesus, however, came to reveal that **God has no favorites. We are all His highly favorite ones,** *fully loved and accepted in the Beloved!*

The simplicity of the gospel is the flat out bold announcement that God, in Jesus, *received all of humanity to Himself.*

Christ died for all, and all died with Christ when He died!

Jesus represents the human race, and God's love extends to everyone!

But let's get back to Ephesians 3:7. Paul says,

"Of this gospel, of this good news, I was made a minister."

"This gospel, and my being a minister of it, is concerning the gift of God's grace."

"This understanding, this revelation, this gospel, this insight into the gift of God's grace was given me by the working of God's power; by the very working of that grace within me."

*"Yes, even to me, though I might be considered by some to be the very least of all the saints, because I at one time persecuted the church, yet this grace was given to me, in order that I might preach, or proclaim, and confidently make known **to the Gentiles** the inexhaustible riches of CHRIST!"*

*"...to make **all people** see what this plan of God was ...this plan of revealing the mystery that was hidden for all the ages past ...this mystery, and the plan to reveal it, was hidden in God who created all things..."*

Verse 10 says,

*"It was revealed IN CHRIST and to our understanding, so that through the church, through the **ekklesia**, through those who see and understand and believe and embrace these things; this concept of the one new man, this new identity in CHRIST, the manifold* (multi-faceted, all encompassing) *wisdom of God might now be made known to the human governmental authorities. Yes, even to the principalities and powers, the governing forces behind the mindsets and mentalities of people, the strongholds of thinking that reign in the heavenly places, in the unseen realms of spirit*

realities, in the very spirits, the hearts and minds of people."

Listen if the principalities and powers, if the enemy knew this mystery, they never would have crucified the Lord of Glory!

If the enemy knew how much you as an individual were associated in Christ, in His death, burial and resurrection, if they knew how totally you were associated and united with the Lord of Glory, they never would have instigated the crucifixion!

Listen, God decreed before the ages Man's glorification!

I am so thankful that when God decrees something it means that He has his mind made up about it!

When God decrees something it means that He is not just playing around! When God decrees something it means that He means business!

Listen, God decreed your release! He decreed the release of your neighbor as well! He decreed the release of the nations to finally be His creation, the new creation!

They stand as free as you and me because of that decree!

*"...to make **all people** see what is the plan of the mystery hidden for ages in God who created all things..."*

Hidden, not from us, but for us!

You know, God remains the creator of all things. **How in the world can anyone challenge God in His right as owner and creator, and Father?!**

Paul says that this mystery,

*"...has now been revealed IN CHRIST, so that NOW **through us, the church,** the manifold,* (the all-inclusive) *wisdom of CHRIST* (so far reaching in its affect) *might NOW be made known to the principalities and powers that be."*

Listen, these things are no longer a mystery to the enemy. Man's redemption is no longer a mystery to Darkness! The enemy knows that his only hope is to keep Mankind deceived and ignorant of what he already knows is a reality!

Listen, YOU are the open exhibition of the triumph that occurred on humanity's behalf, that very triumph that took place in Christ Jesus and translated Man out of darkness and into the kingdom of the Son of His love.

YOU, yes YOU believer, YOU are an open statement of the truth! God wants to translate your fellow man out of darkness into His marvelous light *through YOU!*

146

Ephesians 3:11,

"This whole plan and its revelation, this whole mystery that has been revealed now, is according to the eternal purpose, which God has now realized in Christ Jesus our Lord."

Verse 12 says,

"In Him, or through Him **we** (**all of us**, amen, **the whole human race**) *have boldness* (or confidence of access) *through our faith in Him ...actually through His faith, through God's faith."*

"So I ask you not to lose heart over what I am suffering for you (in terms of all this persecution). *As far as I am concerned it is all for your glory; for your glorification* (so that you can learn from my example and follow my lead in not being bound by Man's opinion or influenced by others in the way they think. I much rather prefer to stick with the truth of the gospel instead of Man's religious opinion so that that truth may be preserved for you and for all future generations through you).*"*

Not even Paul's suffering could bring the truth into discredit!

Oh, how quick we sometimes are to judge someone's ministry. Suddenly, we fail to support Paul's ministry and his posse of grace preachers because Paul doesn't see eye-to-eye with Peter anymore. And now the guy landed in prison, you know, he is such a stubborn guy. If he just compromised a little, maybe they would have released him. If he had just listened to the prophets, you know, when they showed him, by the Spirit of God mind you, that if he goes up to Jerusalem he was looking for trouble. Why don't you stay away from trouble; why don't you just stay in the comfort-zone Paul? No man!

He says,

"Don't lose heart in what I'm suffering for you; for your glorification. Trust me, it is to your glory that I am making such a stand and living the life I live!"

Paul fully understands that the life I now live in the flesh, I live by the faith of the Son of God, who loved me and gave himself for me! So I will gladly do the same for you! He understood that the death Jesus died is revealed in our lives daily, so that the life Jesus lives may also be made manifest in our lives daily and now in your lives also! **So that Man is left without an excuse to ignore the face of his birth when they see in us a letter written by the Spirit of God, to be known and read by all people.**

Why all people?

Because it's meant for all!

Because *"If one died for all, then all have died!"* - 2 Corinthians 5:14

Because in CHRIST there can no longer be Jew and Gentile, the included and the excluded, the religious and the non-religious, the believers and the non-believers!

IN CHRIST there can only be one Man, one new Man: CHRIST. *"...For CHRIST is all ...and in us all!"* - Colossians 3:11

Paul concludes in Chapter 3, verse 20,

"Now to Him who by the power at work within us, is able to accomplish far more abundantly than all that we can possibly dare to ask for or even imagine, to Him be glory in the church and in Christ Jesus throughout all generations, for ever and ever. Amen."

Let's not skip over and overlook Ephesians 3:14-19 either. Let's go back there quickly.

In Ephesians 3:14 & 15 Paul says,

"For this reason I bow the knee before (I salute and acknowledge) *the Father of glory, from whom every family in heaven and on earth is named..."*

Listen, the devil is no longer your father, that's a lie religion has sold us. He is not your real father, your true father ...**never has and never will be!** The only things he ever fathered were lies and deception! So, do not submit to a lie, submit to the truth!

In that same book of John, you know, where Jesus told the Pharisees that they are of their father the devil, in that same gospel of John, Jesus goes on to say in John 3:8 that, *"For this very reason was the Son of Man made manifest, to destroy the works of the evil one!"*

And then, just a few short chapters later, he asks of those same Pharisees that were under the influence of a foreign father, of the father of lies, and acting just like the devil was their father because they had bought into his lies, Jesus asks those same Pharisees: ***"Does the Scripture not say that, 'You are all God's property; you are sons of the Most High?'"***

Therefore Paul now declares in Ephesians 3:14-19,

"For this reason I bow the knee before (I salute and acknowledge) *the Father of glory, **from whom every family in heaven and on earth is named**...*"

"...and I desire that according to the riches of His glorious grace, (through the gospel) *He may grant you to be strengthened with might, through His Spirit, in the inner-man, so that Christ may dwell in your hearts through faith..."*

Christ is all in all, amen. *But let Him be all in you, let Him dwell there in you, in your hearts, through faith!*

How does His Spirit strengthen your inner-man, your spirit-man, your heart? **He does** this by opening your eyes to the truth as you muse and ponder upon the reality and truth of the gospel.

The power of God is released through the gospel, to awaken your heart, to awaken your spirit, your inner-man, so that CHRIST in His fullness may dwell there!

"...so that you, being rooted and grounded in the love of God, may finally have the ability, the capacity in your hearts, to fully comprehend, together with all the sanctified ones, what the breadth and length and height and depth of His love is."

In other words, *"...**to fully, intimately, on a deep personal level, know the love of Christ**** (to be absolutely saturated by the love of Christ) *which surpasses knowledge..."*

It surpasses knowledge. In other words, it is more important, **it is of greater value** than mere knowledge. Hey, this thing is a heart thing, not a head thing. It's not just about knowledge, amen.

The whole purpose of the gospel, the whole purpose of God's Spirit engaging your heart with His truth, with the truth of His design of us, and the truth of His love for us, is:

*"...**so that you might be rooted and grounded in His love** ...**so that you might be filled with all the fullness of God!**"*

Chapter 15

Born Again?

Let's just quickly go back there also to 1 Peter Chapter 1. The reference of our new birth is stated clearly in verse 3. **It is directly associated with the resurrection of Jesus Christ** *so that we may conclude that it was indeed in His resurrection that the rest of Mankind was also born again ...***born anew** *there* **to newness of life!**

Why is the word *"again"* used? Because Man was born in the beginning, born from above, *and now God has restored Man* **again** *to that knowledge* **and that reality.**

The Greek doesn't actually use the word, *"again."* The Greek clearly uses the word **anew**. It speaks of us *"being* **<u>born anew</u>** *to a living hope through the resurrection of Jesus Christ from the dead."*

A **living** hope is a hope that is now fulfilled, **a living reality.** It is no longer merely left in the realm of hope. **We are not hoping anymore for what we don't have, amen. That hope is brought to substance by faith, amen. Faith has brought it into the tangible realm of reality!** Thus it is a **living** hope, **an ever**

living reality that doesn't disappoint ever again, amen!

Hallelujah!

Listen do not get confused in your heads now, okay? This has nothing to do with that other *"born again"* doctrine okay! We are not addressing or summarily dismissing the *"You-Must-Be-Born-Again"* doctrine of the evangelical church right now, okay!

Let me just state it clearly if that will help you: I **do believe in a conversion experience! I do believe in spiritual awakening, or whatever you want to call it. I do believe in that impartation of life by the Spirit of the Living God. But please do not get distracted right now by what you think you know or understand. I am not interested in an argument over definitions right now. There is a greater truth that is absolutely imperative for you to see and know and thoroughly grasp and understand.**

Don't let your mind, or anything else for that matter, interfere with the truth of God, with these truths I am sharing that I know your heart bears witness to!

I can see that I am going to have to go to John Chapter Three before we can go on here in First Peter. So let us just quickly take a look there at that conversation between Jesus and Nicodemus there in John Chapter Three.

You see, Nicodemus and his fellow religious scholars were intrigued by Jesus. And so Nicodemus became more and more curious, because in his heart he came to the conclusion that Jesus knew more than him about spiritual things. Therefore he wanted to meet with Jesus secretly in the night of course, because he didn't want his fellow scholars to frown on his desire to meet and get to know this Jesus fellow. Jesus was a very controversial guy, you know, exactly because of what he knew spiritually. Anyway, Nicodemus came to meet with Jesus and Jesus said to him in John 3:3,

"Unless one is born from above he cannot see (the Greek says: See more) *the kingdom of God."*

In essence what Jesus said was,

"Unless you understand the term or the concept 'born from above' you will not be able to see, to understand, to perceive the invisible kingdom of God, that realm, that dimension God exists in, that place where God lives."

You see, He wasn't talking here about the place we call Heaven but about heavenly places, the spirit realm, the unseen realm of spirit reality. Remember, the theme is THE **KINGDOM** OF GOD. In other words, he was talking about the whole realm of God's existence, of God's domain, that unseen realm of spirit reality where God reigns. In other words, He was talking about *the unseen,* but

<u>never the less existent</u>, **spirit realm**. (See Luke 17:20 & 21 and Romans 14:17 where these concepts are clearly defined)

So let's look again at what Jesus was basically saying:

*"Unless you understand the concept that '**if one is born, one is first and foremost born from above**' you cannot see* (or see more clearly) *the kingdom of God."*

He was saying that **it is indeed the truth that Mankind's origin is from above.**

If that was not so, if Mankind's origin was not from above, it would be very hard for any of us to relate to that invisible spirit realm, that invisible spirit dimension, that kingdom of God, all around us and within us.

He was making it clear that **if one's origin, if Man's origin, is indeed from above, from that other higher reality dimension, that invisible spirit dimension (which He affirms it is) then there should be no reason why we as individuals should not be able to relate to the kingdom of God, because we are in fact of that kingdom, of that dimension.**

In John 3:13 He confirmed this by saying,

"No one can ascend into heaven; into the heavenly realm, into the spirit dimension,

156

unless he first came from there and descended from that realm, from that spirit dimension, namely the son of man."

You see, that kingdom of God is all about what is in a man already.

Jesus was saying to Nicodemus and to us that the things of God remain invisible to us. I cannot SEE it as long as I'm a natural minded man, as long as I'm stuck on a natural plane of existence, as long as I am fenced in and caged in by my senses, to where I only relate to my senses, to what I can see with my eyes, hear with my ears, touch with my hands, smell with my nose, or taste with my mouth.

I cannot SEE the things of God, I cannot get involved with it, because it is outside of my realm of understanding, outside of my realm of existence, outside of that caged in dimension of life I choose to live in. Because as a natural man I can only visibly, tangibly relate to, or be involved with a natural environment. (See 1 Corinthians 2:13 & 14)

For a moment Nicodemus, just like many of us, even as learned as he was had a hard time grasping what Jesus was talking about. We can see clearly from his response that he just didn't understand:

"Jesus, what do you mean 'unless one is born from above?' How in the world would it be possible for me to be born from above? I thought I was born from my mother. As far as I

157

understand, I'm a natural man; I was born into this natural environment. I'm a flesh and blood man; I was born that way, how can I possibly change or alter that reality now? The things you are saying make no sense. I mean the things you are saying are hard to understand, if not impossible to comprehend. I mean, from where I stand as a natural being, you sound like a crazy person. What you are talking about are impossible things. How can I be born twice? I mean, how can I re-enter my mother's womb and be born all over again and come out in any different way than I already am? Even if I can possibly do that by some modern marvel of science, I will just come out the same way! How can I be born a second time and then be different from what I am? There is no way. I mean, even if I were to be able to go back or re-enter my mother's womb again, there is no way that I can come out something other than what I am already. How can I come out a second time as anything other than a natural man, born of flesh and blood? How can I come out a second time suddenly born from above now? It makes no sense. How can I come out a second time any different than the first time? I must not understand your statement correctly Jesus, what do you mean: 'Unless one is born from above'?"

Here this man was, a religiously educated man, an important, upstanding citizen, well respected in society as an educated man, *getting offended* because Jesus is talking about concepts that he knows very little to nothing about. Nicodemus considered himself to be an educated man, an expert when it came to religion and spirituality. There wasn't a topic that could be brought up in discussion that he wasn't versed in. As far as Nicodemus was concerned, Jesus *must be* talking nonsense.

'...I mean, Jesus, come on now, don't offend my intelligence!'

But you see, he couldn't just summarily reject and discard what Jesus was saying either, because he was still desperately in need of some spiritual truth that would introduce him into a new life experience, into a new dimension of spirit-life. Nicodemus was desperately in need of a spirit experience, a heart experience, if you will, that would last. He was in need of a deep connection with God that was an ongoing, continuous life in the spirit, life in spirit dimension that was everlasting. Nicodemus was in need of an experience of real life and love and belonging in his spirit, in his heart, deep on the inside of him, exactly the kind of ongoing, everlasting, vibrant, joy-filled, beautifully powerful life that he witnessed in the life of Jesus and which attracted him to Jesus in the first place. He witnessed in the life of Jesus the reality of an intimate love relationship with LOVE Himself; with God. It was so apparent, so obvious, so beautiful and joy-filled and full of life that he was drawn to this man Jesus like a magnet.

Jesus responded gently by saying in essence:

"How is it that YOU, a teacher in Israel, do not know these things? How do you not understand these things and intimately embrace these things? How is it that YOU, a teacher in Israel, do not grasp that you are a spirit being? How is it that YOU do not embrace that YOU, TOO, are born FROM ABOVE, from another dimension, a higher dimension than flesh and blood?"

And so Jesus, through that little encounter with Nicodemus introduces to Nicodemus and to us, the beautiful concept of *'spirit birth.'* **He introduced our spirit birth, our spirit origin, the fact that we are born from above, that Man has his real birth and origin in God, that Man is actually born from above, that Man is a spirit and only lives in a body.**

And what He was saying in essence is that, **when we grasp that, then and then only can we escape our natural identity. Then and then only can we SEE and partake of the kingdom of God within us: our spirit identity, the very image and likeness of our Maker. Then and then only can we enter into intimate fellowship with God in that unseen realm of the spirit, in the depth of our being. Then and then only can we really, genuinely, deep in our hearts, connect with God as Papa, as the one who fathered us, and loves us with His whole being.**

However, so often we hear these great spiritual truths, these spiritual terms and concepts, these spiritual realities, and we end up responding just like Nicodemus. We try to measure it with our natural minds, with our understanding of the natural world we live in, or with our religious understanding, with our religious doctrines we have been brought up with or were educated in. We try to take that spirit truth, those spiritual realities, and we try to calculate and comprehend and catalog and define it by some religious definition, some specific doctrine, so we can file it in our minds alongside all our other religious knowledge files, *instead of simply embracing it and enjoying its reality.* Instead, we quite often end up losing out on the blessing, the life, the sheer enjoyment of it, the encounter of it, encountering and experiencing intimacy, through that Spirit of Truth, with our invisible, but existent, Father God who loves us.

I thank God that Jesus didn't say, *"My words are pure knowledge and doctrine."* NO! He said that His words were far more than that, far more than mere words, He said,

"My words are spirit and life!" - John 6:63

In the light of that I repeat again: Like Nicodemus, **we would have no appetite for heavenly things had we not originally come from there!** Our genesis, our origin, our start is not our mother's womb! **Man began in God.** In Jesus Christ we are introduced to ourselves again. We are identified in Him, in CHRIST, (according to Ephesians 1:4) by God's design, even before the foundations of the earth. And on that basis, therefore, we were also identified with Him in His life and His death and in His resurrection and His ascension!

"Blessed are you Simon, son of Jonah, I say, you are rock – 'petros' a part of the Rock 'petra;' or a small piece of the Rock that begot you; of the God who gave you birth!"

We must understand that being *"born from above"* as the original language puts it is *the realization that we originated in God*, in the mind of God, and that Jesus Christ is the physical manifestation of that *original design*, and that ***that realization or awakening to that truth is our re-birth*** *into that original life and that original relationship with our Maker; our Father; our Genesis; our Origin, if you will!*

"Unless a man is born from above, he cannot ***SEE***...*"* (- John 3:3 The original word used is *anouthen* – '***see more***') ...*the Kingdom of God."*

The kingdom of God (the reign of God's image and likeness, his character, His love, His person) is made visible again on earth as it is in heaven, tangible in human form, in Jesus, **and in those who *SEE* these things and *BELIEVE*.** Jesus intended for Nicodemus and the rest of us who grasp the conversation Jesus had with Nicodemus to discover that our attraction to Him is founded upon the fact that man is more than the fruit of his mother's womb.

"That which is born of the flesh is flesh." Man's natural features and identity reveals a glimpse of his parents',

But there is another womb that man comes from, the womb of the spirit.

"...that which is born of the Spirit is spirit."

Man's birth is not merely by the desire of an earthly parent, (John 1:13) but **by the desire of God. Man comes from above.** *"I knew you before I formed you in your mother's womb."* (Jeremiah 1:5.)

If man did not come from above, then the heavenly realm would offer no appeal or attraction to him. In our very make-up we are the god-kind with an appetite for more than what bread and the senses (natural existence – sight, hearing, touch, smell, and taste) could satisfy us with. We are designed to hunger for the *"Logos"* that comes *from above,* from a dimension where the *original thought* **remains preserved and intact without contamination.**

That *"Logos",* that *original communication,* that *authentic TRUTH* that comes from His mouth is the *unveiled mirror reflection of our authentic design.*

Paul celebrates the same *"**See More**"* theme in Galatians 1:15,

"God separated me from my mother's womb…"

How did He do it? I mean what does Paul mean? What is he talking about?

He is talking about the fact that He, *"...revealed His son **in** me"*

*"…in order that I may reveal and declare Him **in** the nations!"*

He understood what Jesus said to Peter,

*"Flesh and blood cannot reveal to you who the son of man is, but my Father who is in heaven (He alone can). Blessed are you Simon, son of Jonah, I give you a new name that reveals your original identity. You are rock, (petros, hewn out of the rock, petra, Isaiah 51:1 & Deuteronomy 32:3, 4 & 18.) This revelation is the rock foundation that I will build my identity upon, (my image and likeness) and the strong gates of hades, (Greek, ha + ideis, **not to see**) that trapped man into the walled city of the senses – their natural environment; their natural existence, that shortsightedness or inability to **SEE,** will not prevail against the voice that surnames and summons man again."* (Matthew 16:13 & 17.)

The term *"Church"* which Jesus used for the first time here in this scripture, or *'ekklesia'*, in the original language is a word put together from its root meaning. It is put together from 'ek,' denoting *source* or *origin* and 'klesia' which comes from 'kaleo,' which means *to surname* or *identify by name*.

Therefore, when Paul grasped this revelation, when Paul came to this conclusion, when he understood his origin, **his shared identity and sonship with Jesus Christ**, *he did not immediately consult with flesh and blood.* That means he deliberately avoided the opportunity to get to know Jesus from a human point of view by visiting the eleven disciples who were still alive and living in Jerusalem. They could have informed him firsthand about the life, ministry, parables and miracles of Jesus. But Paul does not make mention, in any of his writings even, of a single parable Jesus told or miracle He performed *because his mandate and revelation was not to reveal Christ in history, but Christ in Man.* It was three years later before Paul returned to Jerusalem, and he only returned briefly to Jerusalem specifically to visit Peter and James, the Lord's brother as we read in Galatians 1:18 & 19.

In 2 Corinthians 5:14 & 16 he makes it plain that he, *"...is convinced that if one has died for all; then all have died, and from now on, therefore, he says, we regard no one from a human point of view, not even Jesus."*

He says, *"Even though we once regarded Christ according to the flesh or from a human point of view, we regard him thus no longer!"*

Then he goes on to say in 2 Corinthians 5:17 that,

*"If, **therefore,** any man **is in CHRIST**, he **IS a new creation.** The old things have passed away (that old identity, that old reality under Adam has passed away)."*

*"Behold, **(realize and believe)** that all things; the entire cosmos, the whole created order has now become new again ...**all things are new!**"*

He says, *"**Behold all things are new!**"*

In the light of this revelation of **us in CHRIST**, and **CHRIST IN US**, one cannot be too surprised to discover that the first believers ever to be called Christians were the Greeks in Antioch who sat under Paul's ministry. I want you to know that **what James, John, and Paul had in common was an understanding that Jesus came to reveal and redeem Man's original authentic spirit identity.**

Now I want to mess with you a little more before we get back to our scripture in 1 Peter. Did you know that you can even be *'born again'* into religious life, into so-called 'church,' into religion, into legalism and into 'rules'? And to be honest, many 'Christians' are. And you start a new life, a different life than before, because you were brought into another life, not by God but by other people, brought into another way of living. But you were still not really *'born again'* into the truth, into an

166

intimate relationship of love, a love-affair with God Himself. You were still not really *'born again'* or born *'from above'* into your spirit identity, into that authentic original life you were originally designed for. You were merely *'born again'* into religion!!

Malachi 1:10 says, *"Have we not all one Father? Has not one God created us...?"*

In Jesus Christ we are introduced to ourselves again! In Jesus Christ the whole human race is introduced to themselves again!

Now that is wonderful! That is powerful stuff! Both life changing and life giving!

"God desires none to perish, but all to be saved, to be rescued, to be made whole, by coming to the knowledge of the TRUTH." - 1 Timothy 2:4

Jesus said, *"**I am the way**, the truth, and the life, no one comes to the Father but by me."* - John 14:6

He said, *"**I am the way**..."* What way? There is only one way: **THE TRUTH!** In so many places and in so many words Jesus said,

"I am that authentic, original TRUTH. I am the light of the world, I am the light of life, I am the light, the enlightenment of every man, I am the TRUTH about Man's design, Man's origin"

He said, *"I am the life…"* What life? There is only one, authentic, original life we were all designed for. In other words: *"I am that authentic, original LIFE! The life Man was meant to live from the very beginning! That eternal LIFE, a life closely connected to God, the father of all spirits, the origin of Man!"*

He said, *"No one comes to the Father except through Me! No one becomes closely connected to the Father except through Me."*

"I reveal the way! Through My incarnation, My life, death, and resurrection, through My work of redemption I am opening the way; a new and living way to you. But I restore that original way, that original life, through that original TRUTH, and the truth of My accomplishment on that cross."

"I nailed flesh and blood to that cross! I nailed what was falling short to that cross! I nailed the fall itself to that cross! I nailed Man's natural identity to that cross!"

"You died there with Me and were raised to newness of life with Me! You belong to Me!"

"That's what I was saying through that cross, IN BOLD, CAPITAL LETTERS! There is no way to make a stronger statement than what I made there!"

"I was saying, I LOVE YOU!!!!"

"I was saying, You can now rid yourself of your old natural insufficient inferior failing Identity, because here I am, hanging in plain sight!"

"I am in your face! Your true one and only spirit Identity is in your face! The truth is staring you right in the face! I revealed the real identity of flesh and blood! Not even flesh and blood can disguise your real identity! Not even the flesh and blood body I came in can sufficiently obscure me from your view."

*"Here I am as plain as day, hanging naked, for all to **see**. Your origin is staring at you! It is an in your face experience! An in your face reality! I am your origin and I will no longer be ignored!"*

*"I want you to look at me as the veil of flesh is being torn off! I have nothing to hide! I have but one message: **I am yours and you are mine!**"*

*"...**I am your origin, your real Identity, your very life!**"*

But before I get completely caught up and carried away in the mind of Christ... ha... ha... ha... let's quickly go back to 1 Peter and finish with that.

Chapter 16

Born Anew to a living hope!

As I said before at the beginning of the previous chapter: The reference of our new birth is stated very clearly there in 1 Peter 1:3. **Our new birth is directly associated with the resurrection of Jesus Christ.**

Why?

So that we may conclude that it was indeed in His resurrection that the rest of Mankind was also born again. *They were born anew, there,* **to newness of life!**

Peter says that, *"God begot us again ...we are born again, we are born anew; the whole world was born anew* **by the resurrection of Jesus Christ from the dead**, *to newness of life, to a living hope..."*

The only reason why the word *"again"* or *"anew"* is used is because Man was born from above in the beginning. **Man is born from above from the very beginning,** *and now God has restored Man* <u>*again*</u> *to that knowledge and that reality, in Christ Jesus, in His work of redemption.*

As I said before, the Greek doesn't actually use the word, *"again."* The Greek uses the word *"anew."* instead. It speaks of us *"being **born anew.**"* Peter says, *"**We are born anew** ...the whole world, the whole cosmos, the whole created order of things, and all of humanity for all time, every single individual is born anew to a living hope **through the resurrection of Jesus Christ from the dead.**"* I remind you again that he speaks of a **living** hope *because it is now fulfilled, **it is a living reality. A right now reality!***

Hallelujah!

We are no longer merely left in the realm of hope. We are no longer just living with some future hope and expectation! **We are living in a right now reality!** We are not busy with some prophetic pictures only. And we do not have to live by some vague prophetic word that still concerns itself with the future. **We are not hoping anymore for what we don't have yet, amen. We are living in a right now reality!**

*"**Now faith, (the faith of God, our faith in Christ, in what is revealed in Him), is the substance of things hoped for!**"* - Hebrews 11:1

*"**It is the very evidence of things not seen... (It speaks of its reality, it speaks of things that exist in the unseen realm of spirit reality!)**"* - Hebrews 11:1

The faith of God revealed, that faith that has now come, that faith that is now ours, that faith has given substance to our hope. It has brought all our hopes into the tangible realm of reality! Thus we have a **living** hope; we are involved with **an ever living reality that doesn't disappoint ever again, amen!**

But let's move on and read 1 Peter 1:18-22. Peter says,

"You know and understand that you were ransomed from the futile ways inherited from your forefathers..."

Why were their ways futile? **Because they were living still in deception and ignorance. They were living subject to Adam's fall.**

He says, *"...You were ransomed from that! Not with perishable things such as silver or gold, but with the precious blood of Christ, like that of a lamb without blemish or spot!"*

*"**He was destined before the foundation of the world, but was made manifest here at the end of the times, for your sake!**"*

*"...**He was made manifest for your sake!**"*

*"**Through Him you now have confidence in God**"*

He says,

"Through Him you now have confidence in that God, the Father of us all, who loves us, who is love personified, and who was manifested in Him..."

"...the same God who raised Him from the dead, and gave Him glory!"

"So that now your faith and hope are in God Himself."

"...having purified your souls by obedience to the truth (by believing and fully embracing and yielding to the truth!).*"*

We are not sons of disobedience anymore, amen. We are sons who have become obedient to the truth.

He says, Verse 22,

"...In sincere love of the brethren, love one another earnestly from the heart."

Why can you now have a sincere love for all the brethren and for all your fellow human beings on this planet, and for the whole created order? **Because your appreciation of the brethren and of every other person that shares this planet with you, is inspired by the knowledge that we all died in the same death, and were all raised to newness of life together.** *Therefore you no longer consider any person from a natural-minded, human point of view.*

"...Love one another earnestly from the heart."

Don't be so quick to find a reason to withdraw your love from another person.

Why?

Because Peter goes on to say, Verse 23-25,

"You have been born anew..."

When were you born? Where were you born?

"...not of perishable seed, but of imperishable seed..."

"...through the living and abiding Word of God!"

He says,

*"You have been born anew, not of perishable seed, but of imperishable seed, **the living and eternally abiding, timeless truth of God**..."*

*"**For**,"* he says, *"all flesh is as grass and all its glory like the flowers of the field. The grass withers, and the flower fades and falls, **but** the 'logos' of the Lord abides forever."*

He says, Verse 25,

"That 'logos;' that eternally unfading abiding timeless truth of God is the good news; it is what makes up the content of the gospel, which was fully proclaimed to you, and made known to you."

What is so good about the gospel?

The good news it contains! What God speaks to Man in Christ is the good news, so that Mankind can see the face of their birth, so that you can see the face of your origin there!

"And as the rain comes down, and the snow from heaven, and saturates the soil, so shall My word be" says God in Isaiah 55:10 & 11.

"It shall not return to me void," He says, *"It shall accomplish the very thing for which I sent it."*

And what is that exactly God? Why did you send your Word, God? Not so that the water can come down from heaven like the rain, only to evaporate or to be dammed up again. No! God says, *"Just like the rain and the snow that comes down from heaven, I sent My word, and it shall accomplish what I want. It shall saturate the soil of men's hearts, and awaken the dormant seed, the seed already buried and hidden there in the ground, awaiting the rain. And that seed will come alive; it will spring forth and sprout and bear fruit, and turn the desert into a fruitful field!"*

He says in Isaiah 55:13, *"Instead of the thorn tree shall come up the cypress; instead of the brier shall come up the myrtle! This shall be to the Lord a memorial; an everlasting sign which shall not be cut off!"*

So what is lying dormant in the soil of people's hearts? **The seed of the cypress, the seed of the myrtle! You see, Deep calls to deep. Spirit joins with spirit, and there is an awakening so that the fullness of Man, in his nature, as the creature of God, can again be on display and so that all of Mankind can again exhibit, in their very nature, the fullness of God! The wilderness may again be a fruitful field; the garden of spices, the garden of the King!**

Hallelujah!

Thank you Father!

Thank you for such a great Salvation! **A salvation that can indeed be underestimated but not exaggerated!**

How shall we escape the consequences of the fall? How else shall we escape darkness? How shall we escape living in it **if we neglect such a great salvation?! Jesus is the only truth, the only way, the only life, the only name given unto us by which we can be saved!**

He is indeed our identity!

Our only true real identity!

Thank you Father!

O Father, these things are overwhelming! So wonderful in comprehension! Almost too wonderful for us when we muse and consider such things:

What is Man that You are mindful of him? The son of Man that You make so much of him? What is Man to You that he dare occupy Your thought-life, that Your mind is indeed full of him? What is Man indeed that You care for him, the son of Man that You constantly take thought of him?

Master craftsman, designer of our lives, Father, our eyes behold the Son. We see Jesus, the mirror of our lives! In Your triumph You crowned us with Your excellence!

Father, and oh, how the prophets searched to taste of the grace that is now ours. They searched to find Your timetable; during what time-period would these things become reality. They searched to see if perhaps they could discover what manner of man He would be, this Messiah of Yours, this Jesus the CHRIST.

But now we thank you Father that these things have been revealed unto us!

Oh Father, and how we beseech the world now to be reconciled to You, to be reconciled to God, **because they are!**

We thank you Father for the reality of this truth!

We thank you for the reality of these things!

We thank you for turning the volume up in our spirits, *the voice of Your appeal!*

So that in life or in death, good repute or ill repute, nothing can diminish the gospel in us, alive in our hearts, *or stop us from communicating that gospel!*

Because there is only one God, there is only one Lord, one faith, one baptism in Christ, in which we have already been baptized by You, one body in which all of us have already been united by You.

Thank you Father that there is only one gospel, one law; the perfect law of liberty, the mirror of Your Word, the mirror of Your truth, in which we see ourselves; our authentic self, our origin, our true real identity, and our redemption back to that reality!

Thank you Jesus!

Thank you Father!

Seal these things within our hearts Holy Spirit ...these eternal spirit-realities. In Jesus Name.

Thank you Holy Spirit!

Thank you Father that You've answered us, our hearts cry, in the secret place of thunder!

We are lost and found at the sound of Your dream!

This utterance of reality ...Your word has been our destiny ...Your word has lived our destiny!

Thank you Father that the image of the Son is the blueprint of our lives!

And that that image revealed, Father, is now our destiny!

Father, in Your Word we've heard a voice we've come to love, bringing to us from eternity, *the success of our design.*

Thank you Father that it sets the seal upon our destiny!

You have answered us in the secret place of thunder. We are lost and found at the sound of Your dream and Your utterance of reality, Father. This gospel, this Word that was revealed, has lived our destiny. It has been our destiny and it has now become our reality, Father!

Hallelujah!

We rejoice in that!

We rejoice in truth revealed!

We rejoice in Your truth, Father, Your utterance of reality!

That image of the Son is indeed now our blueprint and our reality!

Amen.

If you want to delve more deeply into these subjects I suggest you study my books on *"God's love for You!" "God's Inheritance in You," "God's Eternal Purpose,"* and perhaps also the ones on *"You are Innocent!"* and *"Confession of Sin - and Freedom from it!"*

In closing, I urge you to get yourself a copy of *"The Mirror Bible"* available online at www.Amazon.com and several other book sellers. It is the best paraphrased version of the New Testament Scriptures translated from the original Greek text *that I have ever read!*

If you want me, or someone who is part of our team to come to where you are, anywhere in the world, and give a talk or teach you and some of your friends about the gospel message and this magnificent work of redemption, simply contact us at www.LivingWordIntl.com, or you can always find me on Facebook.

If you have been helped or your perspective on life has changed as a result of reading this book, or any of my other books, please get in touch with me and let me know.

I would love to share your joy, *so that my joy in writing this book may be full!*

"That which was from the beginning,

which we have heard
(with our spiritual ears),
which we have seen
(with our spiritual eyes),
which we have looked upon
(beheld, focused our attention upon),
and which our hands have also handled
(which we have also experienced),

concerning the Word of life,

we declare to you,

that you also may have this
fellowship *with us;*

and truly *our fellowship is with*
the Father
and with His Son Jesus Christ.

And these things we write to you
that your joy may be full"

~ 1 John 1:1-4

About the Author

Rudi & Carmen Louw together oversee: Living Word International. They also travel and minister both locally and internationally.

Rudi was born and raised in the country of South Africa, while Carmen grew up in Cortland, New York.

They function in the ministry of reconciliation (2 Corinthians 5:18-21) and flow strongly in the gifts of the Holy Spirit and His anointing to teach, preach, prophesy, heal, and whatever is needed to touch people's lives with the reality of God's love and power.

God has given them keen insight into what He has to say to mankind in the work of redemption concerning the revelation and restoration of humanity's true identity.

Therefore they emphasize THE GOSPEL: IN CHRIST REALITIES, the GRACE of God, the WORD OF RIGHTEOUSNESS, *and all such eternal truths essential to salvation and living the CHRIST-LIFE.*

They have been granted this wisdom and revelation into the knowledge of God by the resurrected Spirit of Jesus Christ, *to establish and strengthen believers in the faith of God, and to activate them in ministering to others.*

Not only are people set free from the poison and bondage of sin, condemnation and all kinds of intimidation, (upheld, strengthened and reinforced by age old religious ideas born out of ignorance) **but many are brought into a closer more intimate relationship with Father God, as Daddy**, through accurate teaching and unveiling of the gospel message, prophetic words, healings and miracles.

Rudi & Carmen are closely knitted together with many other effective Christians, church fellowships, and groups of believers who share the same revelation and passion *to make all people see and understand the truth of the gospel, and to impact the world we live in with the LOVE OF GOD.*

www.ingramcontent.com/pod-product-compliance
Lightning Source LLC
Chambersburg PA
CBHW072342100426
42736CB00044B/1739